At Sylvan, we believe reading is one of life's most important, most personal, most meaningful skills, and we're so glad you've taken this step to build a strong vocabulary with us. Vocabulary knowledge has a direct effect on reading comprehension, and reading comprehension is the foundation of success in all aspects of third-grade academics. As a successful reader, you hold infinite possibilities in your hands, enabling you to learn about anything and everything. That's because the more you read, the more you learn. And the more you learn, the more connections you can make to the world around you.

At Sylvan, successful vocabulary instruction encompasses numerous vocabulary acquisition processes with research-based, developmentally appropriate, and highly motivating, entertaining, and thought-provoking lessons. The learning process relies on high standards and meaningful parental involvement. With success, students feel increasing confidence. With increasing confidence, students build even more success. It's a perfect cycle. That's why our Sylvan workbooks aren't like the others. We're laying out the roadmap for learning. The rest is in your hands.

Parents, you have a special role. While your child is working, stay within earshot. If he needs help or gets stuck, you can be there to get him on the right track. And you're always there with supportive encouragement and plenty of celebratory congratulations.

One of the best ways to master vocabulary is to check one's own work. Often the answer is just a dictionary away, so that's always a good place to start. Each section of the workbook also includes a Check It! strip. As your child completes the activities, he can check his answers with Check It! If he sees any errors, he can fix them himself.

At Sylvan, our goal is fluent and strategic readers who have the skills to tackle anything they want to read. We love learning. We want all children to love it as well.

Included with your purchase is a coupon for a discount on our in-center service. As your child continues on his academic journey, your local Sylvan Learning Center can partner with your family in ensuring your child remains a confident, successful, and independent learner.

The Sylvan Team

Sylvan Learning Center.
Unleash your child's potential here.

No matter how big or small the academic challenge, every child has the ability to learn. But sometimes children need help making it happen. Sylvan believes every child has the potential to do great things. And, we know better than anyone else how to tap into that academic potential so that a child's future really is full of possibilities. Sylvan Learning Center is the place where your child can build and master the learning skills needed to succeed and unlock the potential you know is there.

The proven, personalized approach of our in-center programs deliver unparalleled results that other supplemental education services simply can't match. Your child's achievements will be seen not only in test scores and report cards but outside the classroom as well. And when he starts achieving his full potential, everyone will know it. You will see a new level of confidence come through in everything he does and every interaction he has.

How can Sylvan's personalized in-center approach help your child unleash his potential?

• Starting with our exclusive Sylvan Skills Assessment®, we pinpoint your child's exact academic needs.

• Then we develop a customized learning plan designed to achieve your child's academic goals.

• Through our method of skill mastery, your child will not only learn and master every skill in his personalized plan, he will be truly motivated and inspired to achieve his full potential.

To get started, included with this Sylvan product purchase is $10 off our exclusive Sylvan Skills Assessment®. Simply use this coupon and contact your local Sylvan Learning Center to set up your appointment.

And to learn more about Sylvan and our innovative in-center programs, call 1-800-EDUCATE or visit www.educate.com. ***With over 1,100 locations in North America, there is a Sylvan Learning Center near you!***

3rd-Grade Vocabulary Success

Published in the United States by Random House, Inc., New York, and in Canada by Random House of Canada Limited, Toronto.

www.tutoring.sylvanlearning.com

Created by Smarterville Productions LLC
Cover and Interior Photos: Jonathan Pozniak
Cover and Interior Illustrations: Duendes del Sur

First Edition

ISBN: 978-0-375-43002-2

Library of Congress Cataloging-in-Publication Data available upon request.

This book is available at special discounts for bulk purchases for sales promotions or premiums. For more information, write to Special Markets/Premium Sales, 1745 Broadway, MD 6-2, New York, New York 10019 or e-mail specialmarkets@randomhouse.com.

PRINTED IN CHINA

10 9 8 7 6 5 4 3 2 1

Contents

Checking your answers is part of the learning.

Each section of the workbook begins with an easy-to-use Check It! strip.

1. Before beginning the activities, cut out the Check It! strip.

2. As you complete the activities on each page, check your answers.

3. If you find an error, you can correct it yourself.

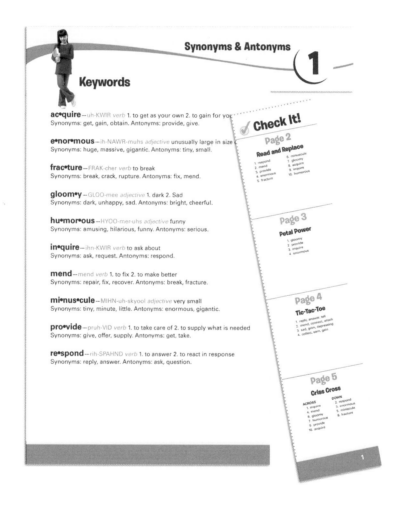

Synonyms & Antonyms

1

Keywords

ac•quire—uh-KWIR *verb* 1. to get as your own 2. to gain for you
Synonyms: get, gain, obtain. Antonyms: provide, give.

e•nor•mous—ih-NAWR-muhs *adjective* unusually large in size
Synonyms: huge, massive, gigantic. Antonyms: tiny, small.

frac•ture—FRAK-cher *verb* to break
Synonyms: break, crack, rupture. Antonyms: fix, mend.

gloom•y—GLOO-mee *adjective* 1. dark 2. Sad
Synonyms: dark, unhappy, sad. Antonyms: bright, cheerful.

hu•mor•ous—HYOO-mer-uhs *adjective* funny
Synonyms: amusing, hilarious, funny. Antonyms: serious.

in•quire—ihn-KWIR *verb* to ask about
Synonyms: ask, request. Antonyms: respond.

mend—mend *verb* 1. to fix 2. to make better
Synonyms: repair, fix, recover. Antonyms: break, fracture.

mi•nus•cule—MIHN-uh-skyool *adjective* very small
Synonyms: tiny, minute, little. Antonyms: enormous, gigantic.

pro•vide—pruh-VID *verb* 1. to take care of 2. to supply what is needed
Synonyms: give, offer, supply. Antonyms: get, take.

re•spond—rih-SPAHND *verb* 1. to answer 2. to react in response
Synonyms: reply, answer. Antonyms: ask, question.

✓ **Check It!**

Page 2
Read and Replace

1. respond   6. minuscule
2. mend   7. gloomy
3. provide   8. acquire
4. enormous   9. inquire
5. fracture   10. humorous

Page 3
Petal Power

1. gloomy
2. provide
3. inquire
4. enormous

Page 4
Tic-Tac-Toe

1. reply, answer, tell
2. mend, connect, attach
3. sad, grim, depressing
4. collect, earn, gain

Page 5
Criss Cross

ACROSS   DOWN
1. inquire   2. respond
4. mend   3. enormous
6. gloomy   5. minuscule
7. humorous   8. fracture
9. provide
10. acquire

1

Keywords

ac•quire—uh-KWIR *verb* 1. to get as your own 2. to gain for yourself
Synonyms: get, gain, obtain. Antonyms: provide, give.

e•nor•mous—ih-NAWR-muhs *adjective* unusually large in size or number
Synonyms: huge, massive, gigantic. Antonyms: tiny, small.

frac•ture—FRAK-cher *verb* to break
Synonyms: break, crack, rupture. Antonyms: fix, mend.

gloom•y—GLOO-mee *adjective* 1. dark 2. sad
Synonyms: dark, unhappy, sad. Antonyms: bright, cheerful.

hu•mor•ous—HYOO-mer-uhs *adjective* funny
Synonyms: amusing, hilarious, funny. Antonyms: serious.

in•quire—ihn-KWIR *verb* to ask about
Synonyms: ask, request. Antonyms: respond.

mend—mend *verb* 1. to fix 2. to make better
Synonyms: repair, fix, recover. Antonyms: break, fracture.

mi•nus•cule—MIHN-uh-skyool *adjective* very small
Synonyms: tiny, minute, little. Antonyms: enormous, gigantic.

pro•vide—pruh-VID *verb* 1. to take care of 2. to supply what is needed
Synonyms: give, offer, supply. Antonyms: get, take.

re•spond—rih-SPAHND *verb* 1. to answer 2. to react in response
Synonyms: reply, answer. Antonyms: ask, question.

✓ Check It!

Page 2

Read and Replace

1. respond
2. mend
3. provide
4. enormous
5. fracture
6. minuscule
7. gloomy
8. acquire
9. inquire
10. humorous

Page 3

Petal Power

1. gloomy
2. provide
3. inquire
4. enormous

Page 4

Tic-Tac-Toe

1. reply, answer, tell
2. mend, connect, attach
3. sad, grim, depressing
4. collect, earn, gain

Page 5

Criss Cross

ACROSS
1. inquire
4. mend
6. gloomy
7. humorous
9. provide
10. acquire

DOWN
2. respond
3. enormous
5. miniscule
8. fracture

Check It!

Read & Replace

READ the letter. Each word in **bold** is a SYNONYM to a keyword. Synonyms are words that have the same meanings, like *broad* and *wide*. FILL IN the blanks using a keyword from the word box.

acquire   enormous   fracture   gloomy   humorous

inquire   mend   minuscule   provide   respond

Dear Ms. Trainer,

I am writing this to 1 _respond_ [reply] to your e-mail. I'm sorry to hear

your elephant has a broken bone. I wish that I could help you

2 _mend_ [fix] your elephant's leg. Unfortunately I do not have

a cast to 3 _provide_ [give] you. My company does not make casts

for 4 _enormous_ [very large] animals when they 5 _fracture_ [break] a bone. Most

people can tell by our company name that we only make casts

for 6 _minuscule_ [tiny] creatures.

I know this must be a 7 _gloomy_ [sad] time for you. I hope you will

8 _acquire_ [get] the cast you need soon. You might want to contact

the Jumbo Cast Company to 9 _inquire_ [ask] about a cast.

Sincerely,

Dr. Bones, President

Itsy Bitsy Cast Company

P.S. I don't mean to be 10 _humorous_ [funny] at such

a serious time, but if you do ever need a

cast for any of the fleas at your circus, I'd be

happy to help.

Petal Power

The petals around the flowers are ANTONYMS to the word in the center. Antonyms are words that have opposite meanings, like *tiny* and *huge*. READ the words around each flower and WRITE an antonym from the keywords in the center.

enormous   gloomy   inquire   ~~mend~~   provide

Example:

break

tear   mend   fracture

rip

1. happy

pleasant   *gloomy*   joyful

sunny

2. take

obtain   *provide*   acquire

gain

3. reply

answer   *inquire*   respond

tell

4. tiny

miniscule   *enormous*   little

puny

Synonyms & Antonyms

Tic-Tac-Toe

PLAY Tic-tac-toe with synonyms and antonyms. CIRCLE any word that is a synonym to the blue word. PUT an X through any antonyms. When you find three synonyms or antonyms in a row, you are a winner! The line can go across, down, or horizontally.

Example:

miniscule

large	(tiny)	gig~~antic~~
~~big~~	(petite)	(small)
(miniature)	(little)	~~huge~~

1. respond

reply	ask	question
ignore	answer	inquire
react	request	tell

2. fracture

break	fix	mend
crack	shatter	connect
join	tear	attach

3. humorous

sad	comical	funny
serious	grim	laughable
hilarious	unfunny	depressing

4. acquire

give	get	gain
lose	earn	sell
collect	provide	buy

Criss Cross

FILL IN the grid by writing keywords that are synonyms to the clues.

ACROSS

1. To ask inquire
4. To fix mend
6. Dark or sad gloomy
7. Funny humorous
9. To give something to someone
10. To get something for yourself

DOWN

2. To answer
3. Very big
5. Tiny
8. To break

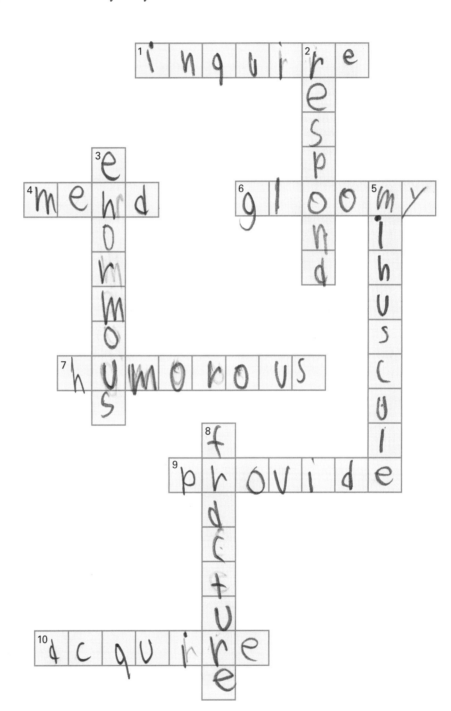

Synonyms & Antonyms

Blank Out!

FILL IN the blanks with keywords.

~~acquire~~   ~~enormous~~   ~~fracture~~   ~~gloomy~~   ~~humorous~~
~~inquire~~   ~~mend~~   ~~minuscule~~   ~~provide~~   ~~respond~~

1. Kendra ripped her shirt climbing the rock wall. Now she'll have to _mend_ it.

2. If you hit a baseball through the window, you will _provide_ the glass.

3. The ring leader will _fracture_ red noses to all the students at clown school.

4. It took hours for Jack and Liz to finish their _enormous_ tub of popcorn.

5. Anna will _inquire_ and find out if the mountain is open for snowboarding.

6. It's a _gloomy_ day when your best friend moves away.

7. We had to use a microscope to see the _minuscule_ creatures living in the pond water.

8. My brother wrote a _humorous_ e-mail that made my parents laugh out loud.

9. If Kate can just _acquire_ the two trading cards she needs, she'll have a complete collection.

10. Max wants everyone to _respond_ to the birthday party invitation so he'll know how much cake to make.

6

Night & Day

MATCH each word in the moon column to its antonym in the sun column.

HINT: If you don't know the meaning of a word, look it up in a dictionary or thesaurus.

1. enormous   _____   a. bright

2. provide   _____   b. destroy

3. humorous   _____   c. query

4. miniscule _____   d. seize

5. respond   _____   e. microscopic

6. acquire   _____   f. answer

7. fracture   _____   g. dismal

8. mend   _____   h. humongous

9. gloomy   _____   i. hand over

10. inquire   _____   j. meld

Synonyms & Antonyms

Blank Out!

FILL IN in the blanks with keywords.

acquire	enormous	fracture	gloomy	humorous
inquire	mend	minuscule	provide	respond

1. A mountain and a blue whale are both _____.

2. To find out if your friend is busy, you have to _____.

3. The sky is _____ when it's full of dark clouds.

4. When you fix your torn jacket, you _____ it.

5. The size of a period at the end of a sentence is _____.

6. When you get a new bike, you _____ it.

7. If you don't wear a helmet and pads when you're skateboarding, you could

   _____ a bone.

8. A funny joke is _____.

9. When you answer a friend's e-mail, you _____ to it.

10. When your parents give you everything you need, they _____ for you.

✓ Check It!

Cut out the Check It! section on page 1, and see if you got the answers right.

Keywords

ap•proach—uh-PROHCH *verb* 1. to move closer to; 2. to speak to someone in order to ask something
Synonyms: advance, move toward. Antonyms: retreat, pull back.

ben•e•fi•cial—behn-uh-FIHSH-uhl *adjective* 1. helpful; 2. leading to good health and happiness
Synonyms: helpful, useful. Antonyms: harmful, destructive.

grad•u•al—GRAJ-ooh-uhl *adjective* moving or changing slowly in steps or degrees
Synonyms: slow, steady, regular. Antonyms: sudden, fast.

im•prove—ihm-PROOV *adjective* to make or become better
Synonyms: get better, recover. Antonyms: worsen, deteriorate.

lo•cate—LOH-kayt *verb* 1. to find where something is; 2. to put in a particular spot
Synonyms: place, find, discover. Antonyms: lose, misplace.

man•u•fac•ture—man-yuh-FAK-cher *verb* to make by hand or with machinery
Synonyms: make, produce, create. Antonyms: destroy, demolish.

o•rig•i•nal—uh-RIHJ-uh-nuhl *adjective* 1. existing first 2. completely new and not copied
Synonyms: first, earliest, new. Antonyms: final, copy.

suf•fi•cient—suh-FISH-uhnt *adjective* as much as needed
Synonyms: enough, plenty, ample. Antonyms: inadequate, poor.

un•lim•it•ed—uhn-LIH-mih-tuhd *adjective* 1. without limits 2. having no boundaries or end
Synonyms: boundless, limitless. Antonyms: confined, bound.

van•ish—VAN-ihsh *verb* 1. to disappear suddenly 2. to stop existing
Synonyms: disappear, go. Antonyms: appear, show.

✓ Check It!

Page 10
Read & Replace

1. approach
2. vanish
3. gradual
4. improve
5. original
6. locate
7. manufacture
8. sufficient
9. beneficial
10. unlimited

Page 11
Petal Power

1. gradual
2. beneficial
3. original
4. locate
5. unlimited

Page 12
Tic-Tac-Toe

1. harm, hurt, worsen
2. build, construct, form
3. appear, arrive, show up
4. lacking, short of, skimpy

Page 13
Criss Cross

ACROSS	DOWN
2. improve	2. original
3. vanish	4. locate
6. approach	5. manufacture
7. gradual	8. sufficient
9. unlimited	

Read & Replace

READ the e-mail. Each word or phrase in **bold** is a SYNONYM to a keyword. Synonyms are words that have the same meanings, like *big* and *large*. FILL IN the blanks with keywords.

approach	beneficial	gradual	improve	locate
manufacture	original	sufficient	unlimited	vanish

From: Farmer Brown

To: Mr. Mysterio

Subject: My Missing Pet

Your assistant gave me your e-mail address so I could

1 _____ you with my problem. Yesterday I watched

come to

as you made my potbellied pig 2 _____. It was not a

disappear

3 _____ disappearance—she was gone with a snap of

bit-by-bit

your fingers. That was quite a trick! I understand that you wanted

to 4 _____ your 5 _____ magic show. Unfortunately,

better   first

I still cannot 6 _____ Petunia.

find

Thank you for your offer to 7 _____ a new pet

make

for me. However, I do not think a pink balloon

poodle would be a 8 _____ replacement

good enough

for Petunia. Any advice you can give me

would be 9 _____. I have

helpful

10 _____ love for my pet.

endless

Petal Power

The petals around the flowers are ANTONYMS to the word in the center. Antonyms are words that have opposite meanings, like *hot* and *cold*. Read the words around each flower and WRITE an antonym from the keywords list in the center.

| beneficial | gradual | locate | original | unlimited |

1.

sudden

quick _____ fast

immediate

2.

harmful

toxic _____ bad

destructive

3.

last

copy _____ final

latest

4.

lose

pass by _____ misplace

miss

5.

bound

definite _____ curbed

confined

Tic-Tac-Toe

PLAY Tic-tac-toe with synonyms and antonyms. CIRCLE any word that is a synonym to the blue word. PUT an X through any antonyms. When you find three synonyms or antonyms in a row, you are a winner! The line can go across, down, or diagonally.

Example:

approach

come at	go to	meet
greet	take off	go away
leave	move toward	depart

1. improve

harm	better	upgrade
help	hurt	decline
mend	damage	worsen

2. manufacture

destroy	produce	build
smash	crush	construct
make	tear down	form

3. vanish

appear	evaporate	disappear
vaporize	arrive	go away
fade	come out	show up

4. sufficient

enough	inadequate	lacking
wanting	all right	short of
not enough	decent	skimpy

Criss Cross

FILL IN the grid by writing keywords that are synonyms to the clues.

ACROSS

1. To get better
3. To disappear
6. To advance
7. Slowly
9. Countless

DOWN

2. Earliest
4. To discover
5. To construct
8. Enough

Blank Out!

FILL in the blanks with keywords.

approach	beneficial	gradual	improve	locate
manufacture	original	sufficient	unlimited	vanish

1. Taylor practiced at the skate park so she could _____ her pipe grind.

2. They _____ candy canes from water and sugar.

3. Shayna will _____ the singer after the show to ask for his autograph.

4. It took hours for Max to _____ his hamster after it escaped from its cage.

5. It would be _____ to put Brad's bike in the garage before the storm hits.

6. Casey watched her chalk drawing _____ in the rain.

7. Please make sure to order a _____ amount of pizza for the party.

8. The tide will make a _____ move up the beach, so we should move our towels.

9. Darren has an _____ pass to the amusement park this year so he can go anytime he wants.

10. The _____ surfboards were made from wood. Now they're mostly made with fiberglass.

Night & Day

MATCH each word in the moon column to its antonym in the sun column.

1. unlimited   _____   a. wanting

2. gradual   _____   b. destroy

3. sufficient   _____   c. misplace

4. manufacture   _____   d. leave

5. locate   _____   e. damaging

6. approach   _____   f. copy

7. vanish   _____   g. worsen

8. beneficial   _____   h. limited

9. improve   _____   i. appear

10. original   _____   j. rapid

Blank Out!

FILL in the blanks with keywords.

approach	beneficial	gradual	improve	locate
manufacture	original	sufficient	unlimited	vanish

1. When you blow out your birthday candles, the flames _____.

2. If you want to be a better dancer, you need to _____.

3. To find your lost baseball card, you need to _____ it.

4. If you want to buy a 75-cent candy bar, a dollar is _____.

5. People who work in a car factory _____ cars.

6. Flippers are _____ to a swimmer.

7. When dogs want to sniff your hand, they _____ you.

8. The number of stars you can see in the sky is _____.

9. The speed at which your hair grows is _____.

10. Your very first bicycle is your _____ bicycle.

 **Check It!**

Cut out the Check It! section on page 9, and see if you got the answers right.

Keywords

bare—BAYR *adjective* 1. naked 2. exposed for all to see 3. empty

bear—BAYR *noun* a large mammal that has long shaggy hair and a short tail and eats both plants and meat
verb 1. to hold up something heavy 2. to keep in one's mind

fair—FAYR *noun* 1. a gathering of people who are buying and selling things 2. an event with rides, games, and competitions
adjective 1. beautiful 2. clean or pure 3. not stormy or cloudy 4. likely to happen 5. not dark 6. neither good nor bad 7. in a way that is equal for everyone involved

fare—FAYR *noun* 1. food 2. the money a person pays to travel by public transportation

heal—HEEL *verb* to make healthy

heel—HEEL *noun* 1. the back part of the foot below the ankle 2. the part of a shoe that covers the back of the foot 3. the lower, back, or end part 4. a person who is not nice
verb to make a person or animal obey

scent—SEHNT *noun* 1. an odor or smell 2. a sense of smell 3. hint 4. perfume

sent—SEHNT *verb* 1. caused to go 2. caused to happen

weak—WEEK *adjective* not strong

week—WEEK *noun* the period of seven days that begins with Sunday and ends with Saturday

✓ Check It!

Page 18

Read & Replace

1. bear
2. bare
3. week
4. weak
5. sent
6. fair
7. fare
8. heal
9. heel
10. scent

Page 19

Homophone Hopscotch

Board 1	Board 2	Board 3
1. fair	1. heel	1. bare
2. fare	2. heel	2. bear
3. fair	3. heel	3. bear
4. fare	4. heal	4. bare
5. fair	5. heel	5. bare

Page 20

It's Puzzling!

A. fair/I. fare
B. week/G. weak
C. bear/J. bare
D. heel/F. heal
E. scent/H. sent

Page 21

Criss Cross

ACROSS	DOWN
1. weak	1. week
2. heel	2. heal
3. bear	3. bare
4. fair	4. fare
5. scent	5. sent

✓ **Check It!**

Page 22

Blank Out!

1. week
2. fair
3. sent
4. bare
5. heal
6. bear
7. fare
8. weak
9. heel
10. scent

Page 23

Double Trouble

1. fair
2. heel
3. bear
4. week
5. scent
6. sent
7. weak
8. bare
9. heal
10. fare

Page 24

Blank Out!

1. fair
2. fare
3. week
4. weak
5. bear
6. bare
7. scent
8. sent
9. heel
10. heal

Read & Replace

HOMOPHONES are words that sound the same but have different meanings. *Too*, *two*, and *to* are homophones. READ the story. FILL IN the blanks with keywords.

HINT: Read the whole story before you choose your words.

bear	fare	heel	sent	week
bare	fair	heal	scent	weak

This morning, I heard Mom yell, "Henry, you had better not be going out in your 1_____ feet!" I said, "Mom, I love my big, furry clawed slippers. Would you rather me go out without anything on my 2_____ feet?"

The slippers came in the mail last 3_____. They were a present from my Great Aunt Irma. She may look 4_____, but once she hit a baseball so hard she 5_____ it flying to the next town. Great Aunt Irma is a lot of fun. We always go to the county 6_____ together, and she even pays the bus 7_____ for me. She sells a magic cream at the fair that can 8_____ any toothache if you rub it on your 9_____. Great Aunt Irma puts a drop of skunk 10_____ into every batch. I love my Great Aunt Irma a lot, but I would never ever buy her toothache cream!

Stinky Skunk Toothache Cream

Homophone Hopscotch

LOOK AT the clues for each hopscotch board. MATCH each space on the board to its clue. Then FILL IN the correct keyword.

Board 1: fair/fare
1. beautiful
2. price to ride a train
3. a place where people buy and sell things
4. food
5. in a way that's equal for everyone

Board 2: heal/heel
1. a person who is not nice
2. the back part of the foot
3. the end part
4. to make better
5. to make an animal obey

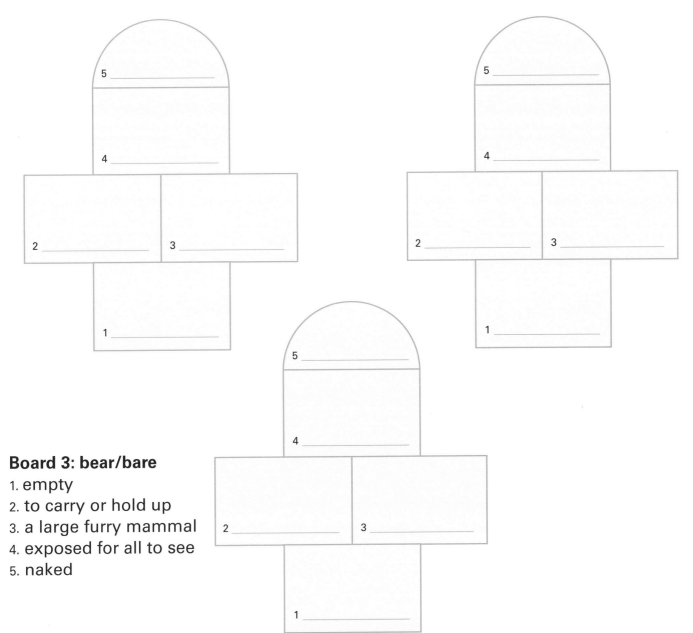

Board 3: bear/bare
1. empty
2. to carry or hold up
3. a large furry mammal
4. exposed for all to see
5. naked

It's Puzzling!

FILL IN a keyword to solve each clue. Then DRAW a line from each puzzle piece to its homophone partner.

You can get cotton candy here.

When wounds get better, they _____.

You find this on your calendar.

If you can't lift a pencil, someone might call you this.

Watch out for this animal in a forest.

Your friend got your letter after you _____ it.

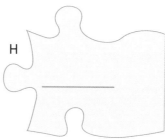

You need a leash to train your dog to do this.

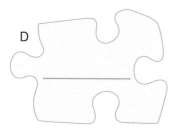

You have to pay this before you get on an airplane.

This fills the air when your dad's baking cookies.

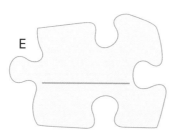

If your refrigerator is this, you'll have to go shopping.

Criss Cross

FILL IN the grid by answering the clues with keywords.

ACROSS

1. Not strong
2. The back of your foot
3. Hold up something heavy
4. Not stormy or cloudy
5. Perfume

DOWN

1. From Sunday to Saturday
2. To make healthy
3. Out in the open for all to see
4. Food
5. Shipped

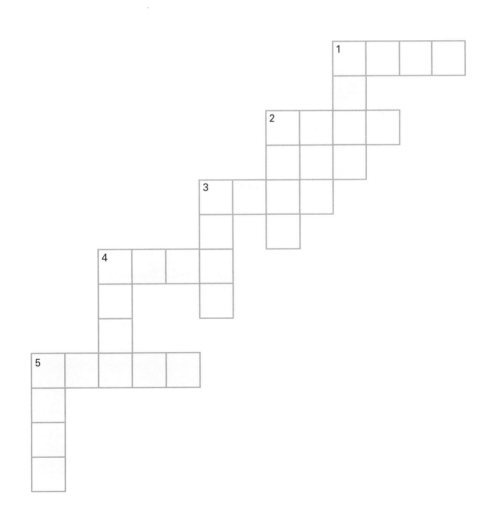

Blank Out!

FILL in the blanks with keywords.

bear	fare	heel	scent	weak
bare	fair	heal	sent	week

1. Jamie plans to sleep late every day during our _____ off from school.

2. It's _____ to take turns with your brother, but it's not always fun.

3. Kristen _____ a box full of toy spiders to her best friend.

4. Eric had to _____ his deepest secret to us during our game of Truth or Dare.

5. The doctors said Jaden's broken leg would take months to _____.

6. Jackson can't _____ waiting for the playoff game.

7. Mom wanted to eat at a restaurant that served French _____, but we just wanted pizza.

8. Everyone thought Trish was _____ until they watched her pick up the boy and lift him over her head.

9. Maya found out that it was impossible to teach her pet frog to _____.

10. Kevin still had the _____ of ocean water in his hair after he surfed all day.

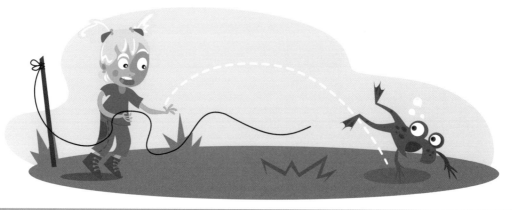

Double Trouble

CIRCLE the keyword that completes each sentence.

1. We should go to the park on the next fair / fare day.

2. Eli's new soccer cleats hurt his heel / heal.

3. Alexa will never throw away the stuffed bear / bare she got when she was a baby.

4. Hannah's favorite band is coming to town next weak / week.

5. Jenna loves everything about the circus, except for the sent / scent of the

    elephants.

6. Matt sometimes wishes his parents had sent / scent his sister to boarding school.

7. Tonya was still feeling week / weak from the flu.

8. Kim liked to ride her horse without a saddle, or bearback / bareback.

9. Our club wants to do things that will help heal / heel the Earth.

10. You can pay the fare / fair at the ticket counter.

Blank Out!

FILL in the blanks with keywords.

bear	fare	heel	scent	weak
bare	fair	heal	sent	week

1. This word describes a place where you'll find Ferris wheels and pig races.

   _____

2. This word tells what a restaurant serves. _____

3. This word describes seven days in a row on a calendar. _____

4. This word describes how you feel when you have no energy. _____

5. This word describes an animal that can catch fish in its sharp claws.

   _____

6. This word describes what you are in the shower. _____

7. This word tells what dogs use to sniff out clues. _____

8. When you talked back, your dad _____ you to your room.

9. This word describes the end of a loaf of bread. _____

10. This word tells how broken bones get better. They _____.

✓ Check It!

Cut out the Check It! section on page 17, and see if you got the answers right.

Keywords

con•tent¹—kuhn-TEHNT *adjective* satisfied with what you have

con•tent²—KAHN-tehnt *noun* 1. the amount of something inside something else 2. the subject or topic covered 3. the meaning or truth of a creative work

con•tract¹—KAHN-trakt *noun* a legal agreement between two or more people or groups

con•tract²—kuhn-TRAKT *verb* 1. to draw or squeeze together 2. to shorten or make smaller

des•ert¹—DEHZ-uhrt *noun* a land that is dry and has few plants

de•sert²—dih-ZUHRT *verb* 1. to go away from 2. to leave someone that you should stay with 3. to quit and leave without permission

ob•ject¹—OHB-jehkt *noun* 1. something that you can see and touch 2. something that is the target of your thoughts or feelings 3. the reason for doing something

ob•ject²—ohb-JEHKT *verb* to go against or oppose with firm words

pres•ent¹—PREHZ-uhnt *noun* 1. something that is given to another 2. time that is happening now

pre•sent²—prih-ZEHNT *verb* 1. to introduce, to bring out before a group of people 2. to give

✓ Check It!

Page 26

Read & Replace

1. desert
2. object
3. content
4. present
5. content
6. object
7. desert
8. present
9. contract

Page 27

Homophone Hopscotch

1. desert
2. object
3. content

Page 28

Blank Out!

1. (ob) ject
2. con (tent)
3. pre (sent)
4. (con) tract
5. (des) ert

Page 29

Criss Cross

ACROSS	DOWN
2. contract	1. present
5. content	3. object
	4. desert

Double Trouble

1. tear   4. dove
2. wind   5. pen
3. bass   6. fan

Read & Replace

HOMOGRAPHS are words that have the same spelling but different meanings and sometimes different pronunciations. The *bill* of a duck and the *bill* that you pay are homographs. READ the story. FILL IN the blanks with keywords.

HINT: Read the whole story before you choose your words. Remember, each word has two meanings, so you can use it more than once.

content	contract	desert	object	present

"Let's go to the 1_____," Will shouted to his friends.

"I 2_____," said Stacey. "It's too hot today. I'm

3_____ to sit in the shade all day."

"Wait until you see the 4_____ I have," said Will.

Stacey took a piece of paper out of the box. "There are some

directions here, but I don't understand the 5_____."

It was a treasure map.

"There's an 6_____ buried under that X," Will

explained. "So are you coming, or are you going to

7_____ us?"

Stacey agreed to go, but first she scribbled something on a

piece of paper. She stopped to 8_____ the paper to

Will. "What's this?" asked Will.

"It's a 9_____," Stacey said. "It says that if we don't

find that treasure, you owe me a day in the shade."

Will shook Stacey's hand. "That's a deal—now let's go!"

 **Check It!**

Page 30

Blank Out!

1. contract
2. desert
3. object
4. present
5. content
6. desert
7. content
8. present
9. object
10. contract

Page 31

Double Match Up

1. f, m
2. b, l
3. c, n
4. e, o
5. h, p
6. i, t
7. j, s
8. k, q
9. d, r
10. a, g

Page 32

Blank Out!

1. content
2. desert
3. present
4. content
5. present
6. object
7. contract
8. desert
9. contract
10. object

Homograph Hopscotch

LOOK AT the definitions in each hopscotch board. FILL IN the matching keyword at the top of the board.

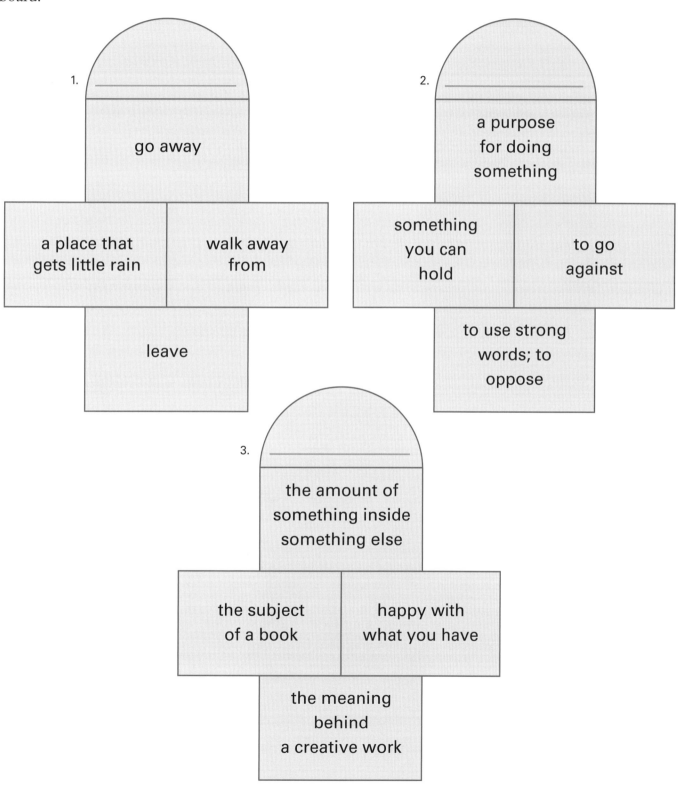

1. _____

go away

a place that gets little rain

walk away from

leave

2. _____

a purpose for doing something

something you can hold

to go against

to use strong words; to oppose

3. _____

the amount of something inside something else

the subject of a book

happy with what you have

the meaning behind a creative work

Blank Out!

FILL in the blanks with keywords. Then CIRCLE the syllable you say the strongest.

content   contract   desert   object   present

1. Kelly made a sculpture out of an _____ she found on the shore.

2. Tim's dog is _____ just chewing on an old bone.

3. The coach will _____ a golden basketball to T.J. at the awards dinner.

4. Jessica had to sign a _____ when she entered the video game competition.

5. Lizards and tortoises live in the _____.

Criss Cross

FILL IN the grid by answering the clues with keywords.

ACROSS

2. A legal agreement OR to make smaller

5. Satisfied OR the material in a book

DOWN

1. A gift OR to show something

3. To go against OR an item or thing

4. To leave OR a dry place

Double Trouble

WRITE the homograph that matches each description.

| bass | dove | fan | pen | tear | wind |

1. Water that comes from your eyes OR the way you rip paper _____

2. Moving air OR the way you spin around something else _____

3. A type of fish OR a low singer _____

4. A type of bird OR the way you went into the pool _____

5. Something you use to write OR a home for a pig _____

6. A person who loves a sport OR something that keeps you cool when you're hot _____

Blank Out!

FILL IN the blanks with keywords.

content	contract	desert	object	present

1. Jake and Caitlin signed a _____ before they started their babysitting business.

2. You should bring a bottle of water if you hike in the _____ .

3. Sarah is the _____ of Baxter's affection.

4. Thea and Joe will _____ their ideas to the band at practice.

5. We should take this thermos camping. It has a _____ of 2 liters.

6. We saw all the kids _____ the playground as soon as the storm started.

7. Carlos would be _____ to ride his dirt bike all day long.

8. We should make a _____ to give to Mom on Mother's Day.

9. No one will _____ if you want to wear your pink boots today.

10. I got a shot before my trip to Africa so I wouldn't _____ a strange disease.

Double Match Up

FIND the two meanings for each word. Then WRITE the letters of the definitions that match the word.

HINT: If you get stumped, use a dictionary or thesaurus.

1. arms _____ _____

2. hatch _____ _____

3. hide _____ _____

4. jam _____ _____

5. kind _____ _____

6. last _____ _____

7. sage _____ _____

8. story _____ _____

9. tap _____ _____

10. wake _____ _____

a. to stop sleeping

b. to come out of an egg

c. to keep out of sight

d. to strike lightly

e. a fruit spread

f. weapons

g. the track left by a moving ship

h. good-hearted

i. at the end

j. an herb

k. a tale

l. the opening in a ship's deck

m. the body parts between the shoulder and wrist

n. an animal skin

o. a difficult situation

p. a group with common traits

q. one floor level of a building

r. a faucet

s. a wise person

t. to keep going

Homographs

Blank Out!

FILL IN the blanks with keywords.

content	contract	desert	object	present

1. This word describes how you feel if you open all your birthday presents and you've gotten everything you asked for. _____

2. If you leave your friend at the dance, you _____ her.

3. This word tells what you do when you show your trophy to your friends. You _____ it.

4. My mom won't let me see that movie. It has adult _____ .

5. This word tells what you cover with wrapping paper. _____

6. The _____ of basketball is to get the ball through the hoop.

7. This word tells what you might have to sign when you start a new after-school job. _____

8. This word describes a place where you hardly ever need an umbrella. _____

9. When you let air out of balloons, they _____ .

10. You might _____ if someone accuses you of lying when you told the truth.

✓ Check It!

Cut out Check It! to see if you got the answers right.

32

Just Right!

You've learned a lot of words so far. Are you ready to have some fun with them?

Synonyms may have similar meanings, but it's important to know which one is the right one to use in different situations. READ each sentence. Then CIRCLE the synonym that best fits the sentence.

1. Greg will need a needle and thread to mend , repair his torn shirt.

2. The mechanic can mend , repair our car.

3. Dad is afraid our old garden hose will fracture , rupture .

4. Victor might fracture , rupture his arm if he tries that trick again.

5. We had to help mom locate , discover her missing keys.

6. Brian was sure he could locate , discover a new species of insect.

7. You can improve , recover your skating by practicing.

8. We have a enough , sufficient amount of food for the picnic.

9. Sal is trying to acquire , gain a computer for the afterschool club.

10. Kelly might advance , approach you to ask for a favor.

11. The coaches will give , provide all of our equipment.

12. They manufacture , invent action figures in that factory.

13. Raina is waiting for you to react , respond to her invitation.

14. Tito will inquire , request about the movie times on Saturday.

15. Nina liked the original , unique version of the song better than the new one.

✓ Check It!

Page 33

Just Right!

1. mend	9. acquire
2. repair	10. approach
3. rupture	11. provide
4. fracture	12. manufacture
5. locate	13. respond
6. discover	14. inquire
7. improve	15. original
8. sufficient	

Page 34

Pathfinder

1. enormous, tiny
2. gloomy, bright
3. gradual, rapid
4. humorous, serious
5. miniscule, colossal
6. vanish, appear

Page 35

Fixer Upper

1. bear	4. scent
2. fare	5. weak
3. heal	

Double Trouble

1. content: satisfied with what you have
2. contract: a legal agreement
3. desert: to go away from
4. object: something you can see and touch
5. present: a gift

Pathfinder

Antonyms are opposites, and knowing your opposites can get you a long way in this game. Begin at START. When you get to a box with two arrows, follow the antonym to a new word. If you make all the right choices, you'll end up at FINISH.

Fixer Upper

Our homophones have gotten all mixed up. READ the glossary. REPLACE each keyword with the homophone that matches the definition.

bare	1. a large animal in the mammal family	_____
fair	2. the money you pay when you get on a bus	_____
heel	3. to make healthy	_____
sent	4. a smell	_____
week	5. not strong	_____

Double Trouble

Write another meaning for each keyword.

content	1. the subject covered OR _____
contract	2. to make smaller OR _____
desert	3. a dry land OR _____
object	4. to go against OR _____
present	5. to introduce OR _____

Sniglets!

English is always growing and changing. Every year, hundreds of new words are added to the dictionary.

Sniglets are fun-sounding words, but they haven't quite made it to the dictionary yet. Here are some sniglets:

purrsuasion—when a cat rubs up against you trying to get some food
eggsactly—eggs that are cooked just the way you like them
rowedblock—what happens when you're too tired to row your boat any further
starecase—a person who won't stop staring at you
whethervane—a device you spin to tell whether or not you should do something
younicycle—your bicycle

WRITE a sniglet from the list to complete each sentence.

1. We were almost across the lake when Michael got _____.

2. Did you ride your _____ to school?

3. They're going to let the _____ decide which movie they'll go to.

4. Dad cooked _____ and bacon for breakfast.

5. Whiskers thinks she can use _____ to get dinner.

6. Mom can be such a _____ when she's angry.

Now it's your turn. Here are some homophones that might inspire a sniglet or two.

ate/eight	dew/do/due	hare/hair	meat/meet
pause/paws	peace/piece	pedal/peddle/petal	which/witch
tail/tale	right/rite/write		

_____

_____

_____

 **Check It!**

Cut out Check It! to see if you got the answers right.

Vive la France!

English is made up of many words from other languages. If you want to master those words, it can help to know where they come from!

Here are some French words that we've borrowed into English. MATCH each word to its synonym by writing the letters in the blanks. If you see a word you don't know, grab a dictionary!

French Words		English Words
1. armoire	_____	a. highland
2. ballet	_____	b. ugly
3. bureau	_____	c. commonplace
4. cliché	_____	d. bio
5. gauche	_____	e. pie
6. grotesque	_____	f. agency
7. plateau	_____	g. awkward
8. quiche	_____	h. wardrobe
9. résumé	_____	i. trip
10. voyage	_____	j. a type of dance

✓ Check It!

Page 37
Vive la France!

1. h
2. j
3. f
4. c
5. g
6. b
7. a
8. e
9. d
10. i

Page 38
Music to Our Ears

1. d
2. g
3. a
4. i
5. j
6. b
7. h
8. e
9. c
10. f

Page 39
Changing Things Up

1. d
2. f
3. h
4. i
5. g
6. e
7. j
8. b
9. a
10. c

Page 40
Let's Eat!

France:	Italy:	Mexico:
croissant	broccoli	taco
fondue	linguini	tortilla
casserole	spaghetti	jalapeño
soufflé	pizza	burrito
sorbet	zucchini	enchilada

Music to Our Ears

Did you have fun in France? Don't unpack your suitcase because you're headed to Italy.

Italy is known for its music, and many English words that relate to music are borrowed from Italian. MATCH each musical word to its definition by writing the letters in the blanks. If you see a word you don't know, grab a dictionary!

1. adagio _____   a. the bass member of the violin family

2. duo _____   b. a musical instrument with strings and a keyboard; music played softly

3. cello _____   c. the speed at which music is played

4. soprano _____   d. music played slowly

5. libretto _____   e. a string instrument that is between the violin and cello in size

6. piano _____   f. a warble

7. opera _____   g. a group of two

8. viola _____   h. a story set to music where the lines are sung instead of said

9. tempo _____   i. the highest voice part

10. trill _____   j. the written lines of an opera

Changing Things Up 🇪🇸

Welcome to Spain! Sometimes words from other languages are changed around in English. Look at each Spanish word and its definition. Then match it to an English word by writing the letter in the blank. When you're done, write a definition for each English word. If you see a word you don't know, grab a dictionary!

1. *embargar*, to block _____   a. vamoose _____

2. *tronada*, thunderstorm _____   b. ranch _____

3. *estacada*, fence _____   c. savvy _____

4. *camarada*, roommate _____   d. embargo _____

5. *el lagarto*, lizard _____   e. lariat _____

6. *la reata*, lasso _____   f. tornado _____

7. *cargar*, to load _____   g. alligator _____

8. *rancho*, camp _____   h. stockade _____

9. *vamos,* to go _____   i. comrade _____

10. *sabe*, to know _____   j. cargo _____

Let's Eat!

All that traveling has probably made you pretty hungry. No problem! Lots of English food words are borrowed from the places you've just visited—France, Italy, and Mexico.

Can you figure out where these foods come from? DRAW a line from each food to its plate. Then go grab a snack!

France

Italy

Mexico

sorbet

broccoli

burrito

fondue

pizza

zucchini

tortilla

spaghetti

croissant

jalapeño

casserole

enchilada

soufflé

linguini

taco

Keywords

pre•cau•tion—prih-CAW-shun *noun* something done beforehand to prevent harm

pre•his•tor•ic—pree-hih-STAWR-ihk *adjective* relating to something that happened before written history

pre•school—PREE-skool *noun* the school a child attends before elementary school

pre•view—PREE-vyoo *verb* to show or look at in advance

re•ar•range—ree-uh-RAYNJ *verb* to put things in a new order or position

re•play—REE-play *verb* to play again

re•view—REE-vyoo *verb* 1. to look at again 2. to report on the quality of something 3. to study or check again

sub•ma•rine—suhb-muh-REEN *noun* a vehicle that operates underwater

sub•top•ic—SUHB-tahp-ihk *noun* a topic that is a part of the main topic

sub•way—SUHB-way *noun* 1. a passage underneath the ground 2. an underground railway

 **Check It!**

Page 42

Read & Replace

1. preschool
2. preview
3. prehistoric
4. submarine
5. review
6. precaution
7. rearrange
8. replay
9. subway
10. subtopic

Page 43

Petal Power

1. pre
2. sub
3. re
4. pre
5. sub
6. re

Page 44

Tic-Tac-Toe

1. topic, way, group
2. historic, normal, school
3. soil, marine, topic

subtopic	precook
subway	pregame
submarine	preview
subtitle	prehistoric
subgroup	prejudge
remake	
recall	
review	
recheck	

Prefixes

✓ Check It!

Page 45

Criss Cross

ACROSS
2. review
3. prehistoric
5. precaution
6. subway

DOWN
1. preschool
4. replay

Page 46

Blank Out!

1. submarine
2. prehistoric
3. review
4. rearrange
5. subway
6. preview
7. replay
8. preschool
9. subtopic
10. precaution

Page 47

It's Puzzling!

1. predawn
2. preexist
3. preoccupied
4. reappear
5. recount
6. refresh
7. subplot
8. subterranean

Page 48

Blank Out!

1. preschool
2. subway
3. submarine
4. rearrange
5. precaution
6. subtopic
7. review
8. preview
9. replay
10. prehistoric

Read & Replace

PREFIXES are groups of letters that come at the beginning of a word. Each prefix has its own meaning. READ the story. FILL IN the blanks with keywords.

Prefix Meanings: pre = before   sub = under   re = again

One day, Tammy visited her little brother in 1 _____.

She thought his class just played all day, so they could get

a 2 _____ of elementary school. But her brother's friend

Adam knew all about 3 _____ creatures like dinosaurs. A

girl named Casey played with the toy 4 _____ at the water

table to see what floated and what sank. When the teacher did a

5 _____ of fire safety, Tammy even learned a 6 _____

she should take in a fire: Get low and go! Tammy helped the kids

7 _____ the furniture in the housekeeping center. She

played Duck, Duck, Goose with her brother's friends, but she got

a little tired on the twentieth 8 _____ of the game. Tammy

and her brother took the 9 _____ home. "I learned a lot

from you today, little brother," she said. "I think you've even

given me an idea

for a 10 _____

for my report on games

children play."

Petal Power

READ the words around each flower. Then WRITE a prefix that could be added to each root word in the flower to make another word.

1.   view

heat   _____   caution

2.   marine

title   _____   topic

3.   arrange

school   way

new   _____   play

4.   cook   view   5.   total

clean   _____   game   type   _____   standard

mature   6.   enter   normal

marry   _____   form

fill

Prefixes

Tic-Tac-Toe

PLAY Tic-tac-toe with prefixes. CIRCLE any root that could be used with the prefix in blue. PUT an X through any word that could not be used with the prefix. When you find three X's or O's in a row, you're a winner! The line can go across, down, or diagonally. When you're done, make a list of all the words.

1. sub

view	topic	caution
cycle	way	marine
title	group	fix

2. re

make	topic	historic
call	view	normal
way	check	school

3. pre

soil	cook	game
way	marine	view
historic	judge	topic

Other Words Created with Prefixes

_____

_____

_____

_____

_____

Criss Cross

FILL IN the grid by answering the clues with keywords.

ACROSS

2. What you do when you look back over your notes to get ready for a test

3. Cavemen lived in these times

5. Wearing a helmet when you skate is a _____

6. A train line that runs underground

DOWN

1. The school where you go before kindergarten

4. What you do when you play a song again

Blank Out!

FILL IN the blanks with keywords.

precaution	prehistoric	preschool	preview	rearrange
replay	review	submarine	subtopic	subway

1. Jason could see an octopus out of the window of the _____.

2. A wooly mammoth is a creature from _____ times.

3. Henry will _____ the play for the school newspaper.

4. We can _____ our desks for April Fool's Day.

5. Francesco was afraid to ride the _____ alone.

6. Tito looked for a _____ of the new video game online.

7. The referee told the football team they had to _____ a down because of the penalty.

8. Maria liked to finger-paint when she was in _____.

9. "Moto-cross" is a _____ in Mark's report about extreme sports.

10. Keira uses sunblock as a _____ when she goes sailing.

It's Puzzling!

MATCH each prefix to a root word. Then WRITE the words in the blanks.

HINT: You can use the same prefix more than once.

pre-

re-

sub-

terranean

occupied

appear

dawn

plot

fresh

count

exist

_____

_____

_____

_____

_____

_____

_____

Prefixes

Blank Out!

FILL IN the blanks with keywords.

precaution	prehistoric	preschool	preview	rearrange
replay	review	submarine	subtopic	subway

1. Before kindergarten, you went to _____.

2. To travel under the ground you can use a _____.

3. People explore under the sea in a _____.

4. You _____ your room to change the way it looks.

5. Before a big storm hits, you buy supplies as a _____.

6. The section titled "Fantasy Games" in your gamer guide is a _____.

7. Before buying the newest game, be sure to read a _____ of it.

8. A _____ shows a clip of a movie that's coming soon.

9. If you want to watch a DVD movie again after it's over, you _____ it.

10. T. Rex stamped around in _____ times.

Keywords

dis•hon•est—dihs-OHN-ihst *adjective* lying, not honest

dis•please—dihs-PLEEZ *verb* to make someone feel dislike or annoyance

dis•sim•i•lar—dih-SIHM-uh-luhr *adjective* different, unlike

non•mov•ing—nahn-MOO-vihng *adjective* in a fixed position, not changing place or position

non•sense—NAHN-sehnts *noun* silly or meaningless words or actions

non•tox•ic—nahn-TAHK-sihk *adjective* not poisonous, harmless

un•com•fort•a•ble—uhn-CUHM-fert-uh-bul *adjective* not feeling or giving comfort

un•like•ly—uhn-LIK-lee *adjective* not likely to happen

un•u•su•al—uhn-YOO-zhoo-wuhl *adjective* not common, rare

un•wise—uhn-WIZ *adjective* not wise, foolish

✓ Check It!

Page 50
Read & Replace

1. uncomfortable
2. nonsense
3. dishonest
4. unwise
5. displease
6. unlikely
7. dissimilar
8. nontoxic
9. nonmoving

Page 51
Petal Power

1. dis
2. non
3. un
4. dis
5. non
6. un

Page 52
Tic-Tac-Toe

1. sense, skid, stop
2. certain, button, easy
3. fiction, cling, final

nonsense	uncertain	disappoint
nonskid	unbutton	dislike
nonstop	uneasy	disloyal
nondairy	uncut	disgrace
	undo	distrust

Page 53
Criss Cross

ACROSS
3. uncomfortable
4. unlikely
6. nontoxic
7. dissimilar
8. unusual

DOWN
1. unwise
2. nonmoving
5. nonsense

More Prefixes

Check It!

Page 54

Blank Out!

1. unlikely
2. uncomfortable
3. nonmoving
4. dissilimar
5. nontoxic
6. displease
7. dishonest
8. unwise
9. unusual
10. nonsense

Page 55

It's Puzzling!

disallow
disappear
displace
nonissue
nonstandard
unaware
unexpected
unfold

Page 56

Blank Out!

1. unlikely
2. dishonest
3. nonsense
4. uncomfortable
5. dissimilar
6. displease
7. unusual
8. unwise
9. Nontoxic
10. nonmoving

Read & Replace

The prefixes *dis*, *non*, and *un* share the same meaning: *not*. These prefixes at the beginning of a word tell you that the word means the opposite of the root word. *Unwise* is the opposite of *wise*.

READ the story. FILL IN the blanks with keywords.

dishonest	displease	dissimilar
nonmoving	nonsense	nontoxic
uncomfortable	unlikely	unwise

Ned was starting to wonder about his friend Paul. Paul told stories, and some of them made Ned feel 1_____. Sometimes the stories were so wild they just seemed like 2_____—like the time Paul said that he had seen an creature with a head like a horse and a body like a tiger. Ned didn't like to think that his friend was being 3_____, but he knew it was 4_____ for Paul to tell these stories.

Ned didn't want to 5_____ his friend, but he knew it was 6_____that Paul would change unless someone talked to him. Ned always thought his best friend was just like him, but now he felt like he and Paul were 7_____. So when Paul told all their friends that he was going to drink rattlesnake venom and survive, Ned said, "Paul, that's pineapple juice. You know it's 8_____." Paul just stared, like a 9_____ object, but later he told Ned that he had never had a better friend.

Petal Power

READ the words around each flower. Then WRITE a prefix that could be added to each root word in the flower to make another word.

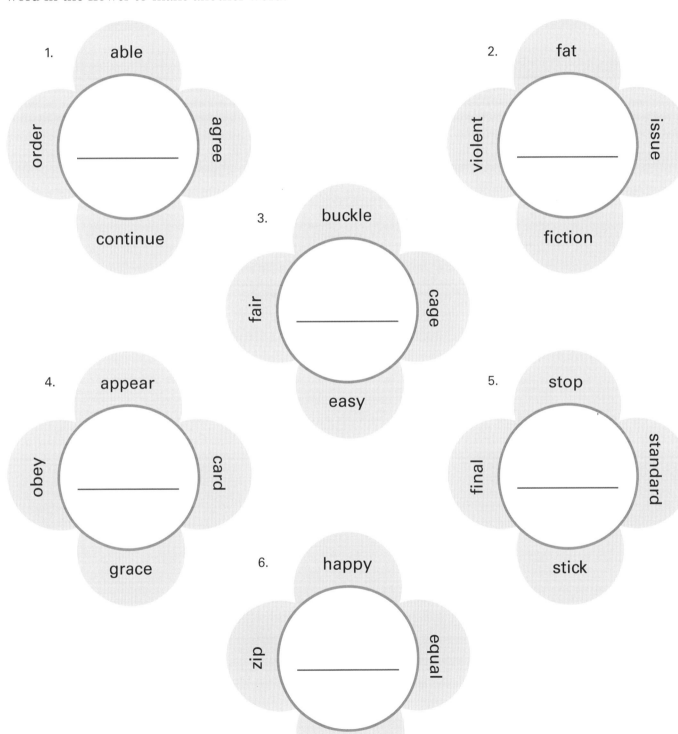

1. able, order, agree, continue

2. fat, violent, issue, fiction

3. buckle, fair, cage, easy

4. appear, obey, card, grace

5. stop, final, standard, stick

6. happy, zip, equal, lock

Tic-Tac-Toe

PLAY Tic-tac-toe with prefixes. CIRCLE any root word that could be used with the prefix in blue. PUT an X through any word that could not be used with the prefix. When you find three X's or O's in a row, you are a winner! The line can go across, down, or diagonally. When you're done, make a list of all the words.

1. non

cling	sense	wind
cover	skid	dairy
fair	stop	fit

2. un

certain	place	stop
button	toxic	cut
easy	do	respect

3. dis

fiction	appoint	like
even	cling	loyal
grace	trust	final

Other Words Created with Prefixes

_____

_____

_____

_____

_____

Criss Cross

FILL IN the grid by answering the clues with keywords.

ACROSS

3. The opposite of comfortable
4. The opposite of likely
6. The opposite of toxic
7. The opposite of similar
8. The opposite of usual

DOWN

1. The opposite of wise
2. The opposite of moving
5. The opposite of sense

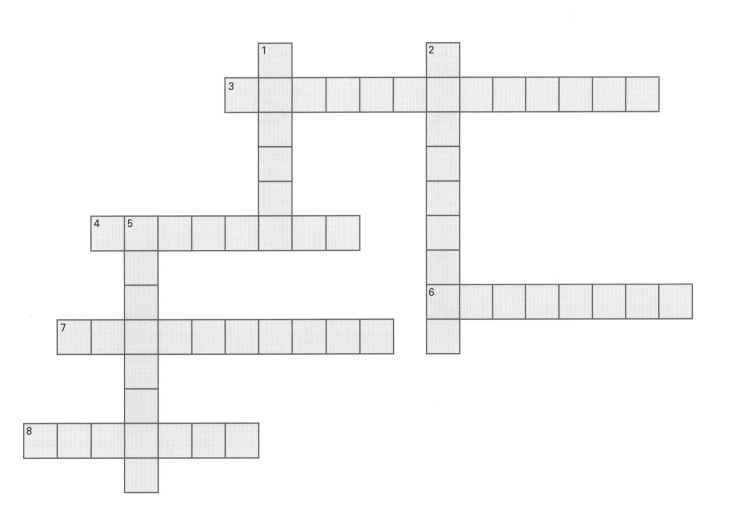

Blank Out!

FILL IN the blanks with keywords.

1. It is _____ that your grandmother rides a dirt bike.

2. A rock would make an _____ pillow.

3. A slide is a _____ object at the playground.

4. Tom likes soccer and his brother likes gymnastics. They are _____.

5. It's a good thing crayons are _____, as my baby sister eats them all the time.

6. It would _____ your friend if you said mean things about her.

7. Lisa was being _____. She said she didn't eat the cookies, but she did.

8. It is _____ to swim during a thunderstorm.

9. A hedgehog is an _____ pet.

10. It's hard to understand someone who is speaking _____.

It's Puzzling!

MATCH each prefix to a root word. Then WRITE the words in the blanks.

HINT: You can use the same prefix more than once.

un-

dis-

non-

place

issue

appear

standard

fold

aware

expected

allow

_____

_____

_____

_____

_____

_____

_____

Blank Out!

FILL IN the blanks with keywords.

1. The possibility of a snowstorm in a desert is _____.

2. Kids who say the dog ate their homework are usually _____.

3. My brother invented his own language. I think it sounds like _____.

4. To put on clothes you've outgrown can be _____.

5. The sizes of elephants and ants is _____.

6. When your friends make you unhappy, they _____ you.

7. Violet-colored eyes are _____.

8. Deciding to wear sandals in the snow is _____.

9. _____ chemicals won't harm you.

10. A car with an engine that doesn't work is _____.

Keywords

care•less—KAYR-lihs *adjective* 1. not paying careful attention to 2. done, made, or said without care

end•less—EHND-lihs *adjective* 1. without end or limits 2. joined at the ends

en•ter•tain•ment—en-tuhr-TAYN-muhnt *noun* ways to give pleasure to or amuse people, such as singing, dancing, and acting

fear•ful—FEER-fuhl *adjective* 1. causing fear 2. filled with fear 3. nervous and easily frightened

grate•ful—GRAYT-fuhl *adjective* having the desire to thank someone

move•ment—MOOV-muhnt *noun* 1. the act of changing location or position 2. the way in which somebody or something moves

pain•less—PAYN-lihs *adjective* 1. not causing pain 2. involving little difficulty

play•ful—PLAY-fuhl *adjective* 1. full of play, fond of playing 2. said or done in a fun way

pun•ish•ment—PUHN-ihsh-muhnt *noun* 1. the act of punishing 2. a penalty for wrongdoing 3. rough treatment

truth•ful—TROOTH-fuhl *adjective* honest, true, always telling the truth

✔ Check It!

Page 58

Read & Replace

1. truthful
2. fearful
3. playful
4. punishment
5. movement
6. careless
7. endless
8. grateful
9. entertainment
10. painless

Page 59

Suffix Hopscotch

1. ment
2. less
3. ful

Page 60

Match Up

1. -ment, d
2. -ful, e
3. -less, b
4. -less, f
5. -ful, c
6. -ment, a

Page 61

Criss Cross

ACROSS	DOWN
1. playful	1. painless
4. entertainment	2. truthful
6. grateful	3. punishment
7. movement	4. endless
	5. careless

Read & Replace

A SUFFIX comes at the end of a word and has its own meaning. The suffix "-ful" at the end of the word *playful* means *full of*. READ the letter.
FILL IN the blanks with keywords.

Dear Brian,

Yesterday, I went to see my

sister Ava's play. I have to be

1 _____ and say that it was terrible. I am 2 _____

that you will come to see it. You would think a musical would

be 3 _____. You would be wrong. The music was

4 _____ on my ears. There were dancers, but there was

little 5 _____. The costumes must have been sewn by a

6 _____ designer. Some of them fell apart on the stage!

The first act went on for more than two hours. It seemed

7 _____! I was 8 _____ when the play actually

did end. They may call it 9 _____, but I like my fun to be

10 _____, and this was hard to sit through.

Sharon

P.S. Please don't tell Ava about this letter—I told her the play

was fantastic!

Suffix Hopscotch

LOOK AT the words in each hopscotch board. FILL IN a suffix that can be added to all of the words in the board.

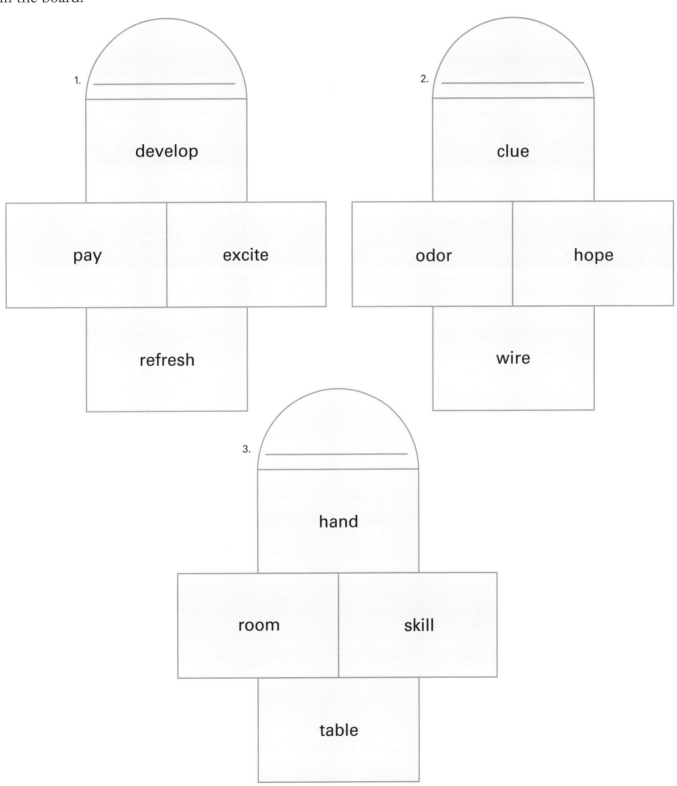

1. _____

develop

pay   excite

refresh

2. _____

clue

odor   hope

wire

3. _____

hand

room   skill

table

Match Up

MATCH each root word to its suffix and write the suffix in the blank. USE the suffix box to help you. Then MATCH a definition for each word by writing the letters in the blanks.

ful = full of	ment = act of	less = without

Definition

1. disappoint _____   _____   a. the act of enjoying

2. waste _____   _____   b. without a job

3. job _____   _____   c. full of respect

4. moon _____   _____   d. the act of being disappointed

5. respect _____   _____   e. full of waste

6. enjoy _____   _____   f. without a moon

Criss Cross

FILL IN the grid by answering the clues with keywords.

ACROSS

1. Fond of playing
4. Singing, dancing, acting
6. Full of thanks
7. The act of moving

DOWN

1. Without pain
2. Telling the truth
3. Rough treatment
4. Having no end
5. Something done without care

Blank Out!

FILL IN the blanks with keywords.

careless	endless	entertainment	fearful	grateful
movement	painless	playful	punishment	truthful

1. Katie knew she could not be _____ if she wanted to land the 360 on her skateboard.

2. Scary movies are his favorite form of _____.

3. Lee had to clean the garage as his _____ for not doing his chores.

4. The ocean looks _____ when you're standing on the shore.

5. Puppies are always running and jumping. They are very _____ creatures.

6. If you are _____ when you eat pizza, you could end up with a shirt full of sauce.

7. The doctor said the shot would be _____, but it did hurt a little.

8. Yolanda liked to sit on the roof of her building and watch the _____ of the crowd below.

9. Dad said Jared won't get punished if he is _____ about what happened.

10. Briana is _____ for the inventor of the jelly bean. It's her favorite snack!

It's Puzzling!

MATCH each suffix to a root word. Then WRITE the words in the blanks.

HINT: You can use the same suffix more than once.

enjoy   -less

peace   -ful

flaw   -ment

mouth

develop

love

state

coat

_____

_____

_____

_____

_____

_____

_____

Blank Out!

FILL IN the blanks with keywords.

careless	endless	entertainment	fearful	grateful
movement	painless	playful	punishment	truthful

1. This word is another word for popular books, movies, and music.

   _____

2. This word describes how you feel when someone does something nice for you.

   _____

3. This word tells what you might get if you don't follow your parents' rules.

   _____

4. This word describes the way you wish every visit to the dentist will be.

   _____

5. This word describes how you might feel face to face with a great white shark.

   _____

6. This word describes the universe.

   _____

7. This word describes what you might have been if you knocked over a bottle of juice.

   _____

8. This word tells what you should be if you want people to believe you.

   _____

9. This word describes what you can see if you watch a butterfly's wings as it flies.

   _____

10. This word tells how you might feel when you're at the park with your friends.

   _____

Keywords

bright•ly—BRIT-lee *adverb* 1. in a way that gives off a lot of light 2. in a way that seems happy and cheerful

damp•ness—DAMP-nuhs *noun* the quality of being slightly wet

feath•er•y—FEHTH-uh-ree *adjective* 1. like a feather 2. covered in feathers

fi•nal•ly—FIN-uhl-ee *adverb* 1. after a long period of time 2. happening at the end or last

loud•ness—LOWD-nuhs *noun* 1. the degree of volume of sound

re•cent•ly—REES-uhnt-lee *adverb* relating to a time not long ago

shad•ow•y—SHAD-oh-ee *adjective* 1. full of shadows 2. not clearly seen 3. not realistic

sly•ness—SLI-nuhs *noun* the quality of being sneaky or smart at hiding one's goals

sneak•y—SNEE-kee *adjective* doing things in a secret and sometimes unfair way

speed•i•ly—SPEED-uhl-ee *adverb* with quickness

✓ Check It!

Page 66
Read & Replace

1. recently
2. shadowy
3. feathery
4. slyness
5. sneaky
6. dampness
7. finally
8. brightly
9. loudness
10. speedily

Page 67
Suffix Hopscotch

1. ness
2. y
3. ly

Page 68
Match Up

1. buttery: like butter
2. deafness: the state of being deaf
3. wisely: in the manner of one who is wise
4. fitness: the state of being fit
5. totally: relating to the total
6. rainy: wet with rain

Page 69
Criss Cross

ACROSS	DOWN
2. brightly	1. finally
3. dampness	4. sneaky
6. recently	5. loudness
8. slyness	7. feathery
10. speedily	9. shadowy

 **Check It!**

Page 70

Blank Out!

1. brightly
2. feathery
3. loudness
4. finally
5. slyness
6. speedily
7. dampness
8. sneaky
9. recently
10. shadowy

Page 71

It's Puzzling!

absently
forgetfulness
pushy
sameness
scratchy
squirmy
stately
weekly

Page 72

Blank Out!

1. feathery
2. shadowy
3. recently
4. sneaky
5. dampness
6. loudness
7. speedily
8. finally
9. slyness
10. brightly

Read & Replace

READ the field notes. FILL IN the blanks with keywords.

brightly	dampness	feathery	finally	loudness
recently	shadowy	slyness	sneaky	speedily

Field Notes

1_____ I made a most amazing discovery. I was exploring the 2_____ depths of a remote rainforest when I saw a creature dash through the leaves. All I could see was its 3_____ tail. I had never seen a tail quite like it before. I wanted to catch the creature so I could observe it more closely. I was sure my partner and I could use our 4_____ to trick the creature. We created a 5_____ plan. We believed that the creature liked the 6_____ of the rainforest floor. We covered our bodies with moss and spread out on the ground. We were thrilled when we 7_____ saw the creature's 8_____ colored feathers. We quickly grabbed it in our hands. Unfortunately the 9_____ of the creature's call shocked us. It sounded just like a fog horn! My partner and I grabbed our ears, and when we did, the creature 10_____ escaped from our hands.

Suffix Hopscotch

LOOK AT the root words in each hopscotch board. FILL IN a suffix that can be added to all of the words in the board.

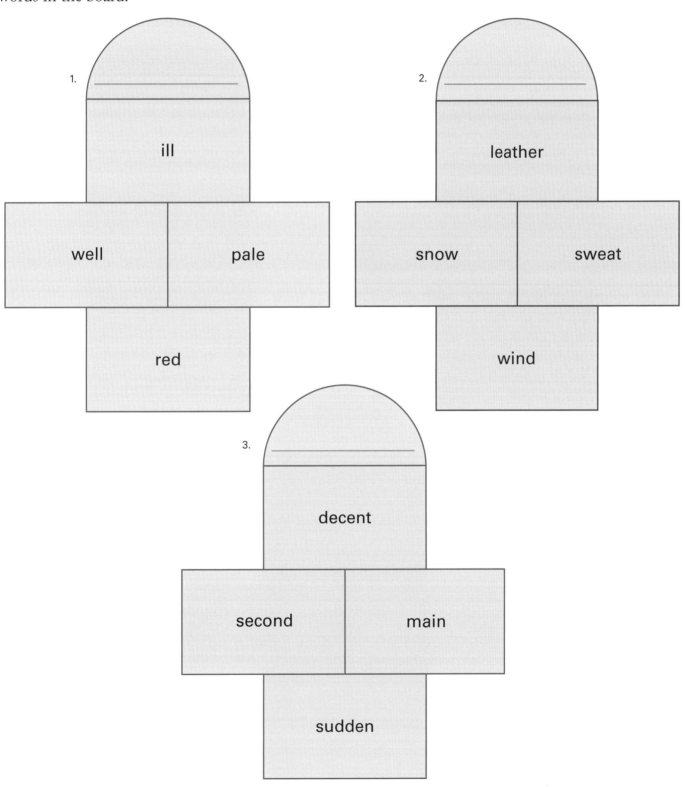

1.

ill

well   pale

red

2.

leather

snow   sweat

wind

3.

decent

second   main

sudden

More Suffixes

Match Up

MATCH each word to a suffix. Then USE the suffix box to help you WRITE a definition for each word.

> -ly = in the manner of; relating to   -ness = state of
>
> -y = state, condition, or result of

	Root	Suffix	Word
1.	butter	ly	_____
2.	deaf	y	_____
3.	wise	ness	_____
4.	fit	ly	_____
5.	total	y	_____
6.	rain	ness	_____

Definitions

1. _____

2. _____

3. _____

4. _____

5. _____

6. _____

Criss Cross

FILL IN the grid by answering the clues with keywords.

ACROSS

2. In a cheerful manner

3. The state of being slightly wet

6. Happening not long ago

8. The quality of being smart at hiding one's motives

10. With quickness

DOWN

1. At last

4. In a secret way

5. The degree of volume of a sound

7. Like a feather

9. Resembling a shadow

Blank Out!

FILL IN the blanks with keywords.

1. The full moon _____ lights up the sky.

2. Valerie is making _____ wings for her costume.

3. The team was excited to hear the _____ of the crowd.

4. It's always sad when summer is _____ over.

5. Martin used his _____ to play an April Fool's prank on his best friend.

6. Carol rode her bike _____ down the hill.

7. The _____ of the basement gave Anna a chill.

8. Paul's cat was being _____ when it crept up on my dog.

9. Brynn could tell the chocolates were not bought _____.

   They tasted stale.

10. Billy was scared to walk in the _____ forest.

It's Puzzling!

MATCH each suffix to a root word. Then WRITE the words in the blanks.

HINT: You can use the same suffix more than once.

absent   -y

push   -ness

forgetful   -ly

scratch

week

same

state

squirm

_____

_____

_____

_____

_____

_____

_____

Blank Out!

FILL IN the blanks with keywords.

1. This word describes most birds. _____

2. This word tells what an alley looks like at night. _____

3. This word tells when you ate breakfast if you just finished it an hour ago.

   _____

4. This word describes the way you act when you play a trick on your sister.

   _____

5. This word tells about the moisture in the air on a cold morning. _____

6. This word tells what fills a room when you shout out the words to your favorite

   song. _____

7. This word tells how you'd want to run in a race. _____

8. This word tells when the package you've been waiting for actually arrives.

   _____

9. This word tells what you need to use to find out a secret your best friend doesn't

   want to tell you. _____

10. This word describes how you might smile when you find out you're going

    somewhere great on vacation. _____

Pick the One!

Think you've got your prefixes straight? It's time to check your skills. LOOK AT each group of words. CIRCLE the actual English word in each row.

1.	premarine	nonmarine	submarine
2.	discaution	precaution	uncaution
3.	replay	subplay	unplay
4.	preschool	reschool	subschool
5.	nonsense	subsense	unsense
6.	disway	unway	subway
7.	recomfortable	subcomfortable	uncomfortable
8.	prelikely	relikely	unlikely
9.	subplease	displease	unpleased
10.	rehonest	prehonest	dishonest

Combo Mambo

WRITE all the words you can make by adding the prefixes to the root words.

dis-   non-   pre-   re-   sub-   un-

1. view _____

2. play _____

3. arrange _____

4. moving _____

Pick the One!

Now it's time to test your knowledge of suffixes. You know the rules—
just CIRCLE the actual English words. Ready, set, go!

1. finalless   finalment   finally

2. dampful   dampness   dampy

3. moveless   movely   movement

4. shadowful   shadowness   shadowy

5. sneakly   sneaky   sneakful

6. playless   playly   playful

Combo Mambo

WRITE all the words you can make by adding the suffixes to the root words.

ful	less	ly	ment	ness	y

1. feather   _____

2. bright   _____

3. care   _____

4. sly   _____

5. loud   _____

6. pain   _____

Pathfinder

Think you know your prefixes and suffixes pretty well? Then you'll have no problem with this game. Begin at START. When you get to a box with two arrows, pick the prefix or suffix that you can add to the root word. If you make all the right choices, you'll end up at FINISH.

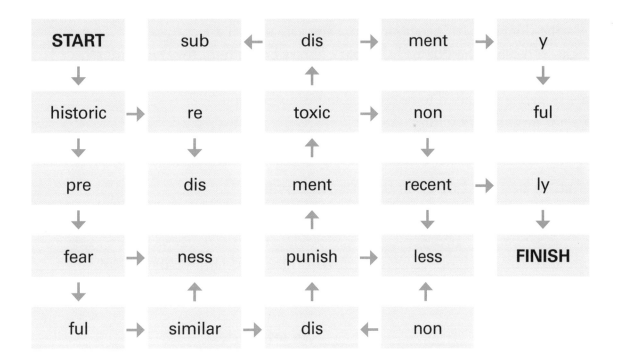

Sniglets!

Are you ready for some more sniglet fun? Remember, sniglets are fun-sounding words that haven't quite made it to the dictionary yet. Here are some sniglets made with the prefixes and suffixes you just reviewed.

snackful—when you've eaten so many snacks that you can't eat any more
predream—the things you think about before you actually fall asleep
nonreturner—a person who doesn't bring back library books until they're overdue
subscratch—the act of raking through the bottom of a backpack in search of a missing item
unfriend—someone who used to be a friend but is no longer
wowless—not thrilling or exciting

WRITE a singlet from the list to complete each sentence.

1. Violet had to pay a lot of fines because she was a _____.

2. Let me just _____ to see if I can find a piece of gum.

3. Sam became my _____ when he told Helen my secret.

4. We held our stomachs and groaned in pain because we were _____.

5. The concert was so _____ we left early.

6. I had so many _____ that I couldn't fall asleep.

Now it's your turn. Here are some prefixes and suffixes you can use to create more sniglets.

Prefixes	Suffixes
hyper- = over, above	-ation = action
mono- = one	-ize = cause
poly- = many	-ism = belief
tele- = distance	-ory = a place for

It's a Zoo in Here!

Other ancient cultures have had a big influence on the English language. In fact, many of the animals found in North and South America wouldn't have the names they have now if it weren't for the people who have been living here for thousands of years. MATCH each animal name to its original name.

1.	moose	a.	tucana
2.	muskrat	b.	coyotl
3.	opossum	c.	móskwas
4.	raccoon	d.	apasum
5.	skunk	e.	iwana
6.	coyote	f.	squnck
7.	alpaca	g.	allpaka
8.	jaguar	h.	moz
9.	iguana	i.	iaguara
10.	toucan	j.	arahkun

✓ Check It!

Page 77

It's a Zoo Here!

1. h
2. c
3. d
4. j
5. f
6. b
7. g
8. i
9. e
10. a

Page 78

A Closet Full of Words

India:
bandana
dungaree
cashmere

Americas:
moccasin
poncho
anorak

Persia:
pajamas
shawl
khaki

Page 79

It's Greek to Me

1. metamorphosis
2. dialogue
3. humanoid
4. microphone
5. pedophobia
6. thermometer
7. pediatrician
8. autopilot
9. anticrime
10. geology
11. geomagnetism
12. philanthropy

Page 80

When in Rome

1. international
2. defrost
3. transform
4. postwar
5. molecule
6. tractor
7. divert
8. coauthor
9. likable
10. aquarium
11. pendulum
12. transport

A Closet Full of Words

Did you know that every time you open your closet, you're seeing an ancient world of words? Many English clothing words are borrowed from the places where the clothes were first worn.

Can you figure out which place each type of clothing comes from? MATCH each word to a hanger. What ancient culture are you wearing today?

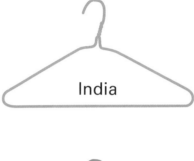
India

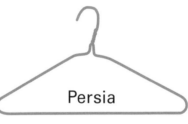
Persia

the Americas

cashmere

khaki

poncho

pajamas

bandana

anorak

shawl

moccasin

dungaree

It's Greek to Me

It's time to travel again, but now we're going back in time. The English language is full of prefixes, suffixes, and roots that are borrowed from ancient Greek.

WRITE a prefix, suffix, or root in the blanks to complete each word.

Prefixes	Roots	Suffixes
anti- = without	anthrop = human	-logue = to speak
auto- = self, same	morph = form	-logy = study of
geo- = earth	ped = child	-oid = shape or form
thermo- = heat	phone = sound	-phobia = fear of

1. A change of form   **meta** __ __ __ __ __ **osis**

2. Words that are spoken between characters   **dia** __ __ __ __ __

3. A creature that has the appearance of a human   **human** __ __ __

4. A tool that makes things sound loud   **micro** __ __ __ __ __

5. A fear of children   **pedo** __ __ __ __ __ __

6. A tool that measures heat   __ __ __ __ __ __ **meter**

7. A doctor who takes care of children   __ __ __ **iatrician**

8. A tool that helps a plane fly by itself   __ __ __ __ **pilot**

9. Something that is against crime   __ __ __ __ **crime**

10. The study of the Earth   **geo** __ __ __ __

11. The magnetic properties of the Earth   __ __ __ **magnetism**

12. A desire to help humanity   **phil** __ __ __ __ __ __ __ **y**

When in Rome

Let's go back to Italy—more than two thousand years ago. That's when they used some of the words that English has borrowed from ancient Latin.

WRITE a prefix, suffix, or root in the blanks to complete each word.

Prefixes	Roots	Suffixes
co- = together	pend = to hang	-able = capable or worthy of
de- = away, off	port = carry	-arium = place for
inter- = between, among	tract = to pull or drag	-cule = little
post- = after	vert = turn	-form = having the shape of

1. Something between or among several countries   __ __ __ __ __ **national**

2. To remove ice or frost   __ __ **frost**

3. To change the shape of   **trans** __ __ __ __

4. After a war   __ __ __ __ **war**

5. The smallest part of something   **mole** __ __ __ __

6. A vehicle that pulls heavy loads   __ __ __ __ __ **or**

7. To change or turn something's path   **di** __ __ __ __

8. To write a book with someone else   __ __ **author**

9. Someone who is worthy of being liked   **lik** __ __ __ __

10. A place to keep sea creatures   **aqu** __ __ __ __ __

11. A hanging weight   __ __ __ __ **ulum**

12. To carry something across one place to another   **trans** __ __ __ __

Keywords

au•di•ble—AW-duh-buhl *adjective* able to be heard

au•di•ence—AW-dee-uhns *noun* a group that listens or watches

au•di•o—AW-dee-oh *adjective* 1. relating to sound that can be heard 2. relating to the recording or reproduction of sound

au•di•tion—aw-DIHSH-uhn *noun* 1. the sense of hearing 2. a test performance by a musician, singer, dancer, or actor

au•di•to•ri•um—awd-ih-TOHR-ee-uhm *noun* a building, or the area of a building, where the audience sits

dic•tate—DIHK-tayt *verb* 1. to speak or read for someone to write down 2. to give orders or rule over

dic•ta•tor—DIHK-tay-ter *noun* a leader who rules with total power over others

dic•tion•ar•y—DIHK-shuh-nehr-ee *noun* a reference book that lists words in alphabetical order and explains their meanings

pre•dict—prih-DIHKT *verb* to tell what is going to happen in the future

ver•dict—VUHR-dihkt *noun* 1. the decision a jury reaches together 2. an opinion about something

✔ **Check It!**

Page 82

Read & Replace

1. auditorium
2. predict
3. audition
4. dictator
5. audio
6. audible
7. verdict
8. dictate
9. audience
10. dictionary

Page 83

Root It Out

1. dictator
2. auditorium
3. verdict
4. audible
5. dictionary
6. audio
7. predict
8. audience
9. dictate
10. audition

Page 84

Combo Mambo

1. audiovisual: relating to sound and vision
2. audit: to tell the details of
3. auditory: relating to the sense of hearing
4. diction: the clearness with which someone says words when speaking
5. indict: to say formally that someone has committed a crime.
6. contradict: to say that something is not true, or say that the opposite is true

Read & Replace

ROOTS are groups of letters that can be found at the beginning, middle, or end of a word. Each root has its own meaning. The root *aud* at the beginning of the word *audience* means *hear*. The root *dict* at the end of the word *predict* means *say*. READ the story. FILL IN the blanks with keywords.

audible	audience	audio	audition	auditorium
dictate	dictator	dictionary	predict	verdict

Neil's knees were shaking as he walked into the 1_____.
He couldn't 2_____ how the band would feel about him, and he was nervous that his 3_____ wouldn't go well.

Neil watched as the band's manager barked orders at everyone. "This guy is a real 4_____," he thought.

When it was his turn, Neil started to sing, but the 5_____ knob on the microphone was turned too low. Someone fixed it so that Neil's voice was 6_____. Neil sang a few lines. "Enough!" yelled the manager. "Have you got anything else to show us?"

Neil waited for hours to hear the band's 7_____. When they said Neil had been chosen to be a member, he could hardly believe it. But Neil knew he could never listen to anyone 8_____ the way he should sing. He'd rather wait for his chance to sing in front of a big 9_____. He turned to the manager and said, "You need to learn about manners. You can start by looking in the 10_____ under the letter 'M.'" Then he proudly walked away.

Root It Out

READ each definition. WRITE the missing root letters in the blanks.

HINT: Match the **bold** words in each definition to a root.

aud = hear   _dict_ = say

1. Someone who **says** what other people should do: ___ ___ ___ ___ ator

2. A place where you can **hear** school announcements: ___ ___ ___ itorium

3. The jury foreman **says** the jury's decision or: ver ___ ___ ___ ___

4. If you can **hear** a whisper, it's ___ ___ ___ ible

5. A book that **tells** where words come from and what

   they mean: ___ ___ ___ ___ ionary

6. The track of sound you can **hear** on a movie: ___ ___ ___ io

7. What a fortuneteller does when she **says** what will

   happen next year: pre ___ ___ ___ ___

8. The people who **hear** a band play: ___ ___ ___ ience

9. When you **say** your notes to a friend who copies

   them down, you ___ ___ ___ ___ ate

10. When someone **hears** you play drums to tell if you

    are good enough join the band, it is an ___ ___ ___ ition

Combo Mambo

MATCH a word or ending in an orange box to a root in a yellow box to make a word. WRITE the word in the root box. Then LOOK UP the definition for each word and WRITE it in a sentence.

aud/audio = hear   *dict* = say or tell

| ion | in | visual | contra | it | itory |

AUD/AUDIO

_____

_____

_____

DICT

_____

_____

_____

Criss Cross

FILL IN the grid by answering the clues with keywords.

ACROSS

3. The crowd at a concert
6. The place where you watch the school play
7. A sound that you can hear
8. A leader who makes all the rules

DOWN

1. To say that something will happen before it does
2. An opinion about something
4. A short performance to try out for something
5. Relating to sound

Blank Out!

FILL IN the blanks with keywords.

audible	audience	audio	audition	auditorium
dictate	dictator	dictionary	predict	verdict

1. Dolphins make sounds that are _____ underwater.

2. We can meet in the _____ to practice for the talent show.

3. I _____ that it will be sunny tomorrow.

4. It's hard to be friends with Peter. He likes to _____ everything we do.

5. The _____ was very quiet during the tennis match.

6. Lauren looked in the _____ to find the meaning of the word audiologist.

7. Lucas can't wait to hear the coach's _____ about who will make the team.

8. It's fun when Mom plays an _____ book for us in the car.

9. No one will want to be friends with you if you act like a _____.

10. Tina practiced for days to get ready for her big _____.

It's Puzzling!

MATCH a prefix, root, and suffix together to form a word. Then WRITE the words in the blanks.

HINT: You can use the same prefix, root, or suffix more than once.

Prefixes

Roots

Suffixes

pre-

aud

-ible

_____

_____

_____

in-

dict

-ion

_____

_____

_____

contra-

-able

Blank Out!

FILL IN the blanks with keywords.

1. This word describes the bossiest person you know. _____

2. This word describes the voice on the other end of the telephone.

    _____

3. This book can help you learn to pronounce *glockenspiel*. _____

4. When you guess which team is going to win tomorrow's game,

    you _____.

5. The fans who are watching the game on television. _____

6. Your MP3 player is an _____ device.

7. This is what you need to do to try out for the chorus. _____

8. This is what the jury says when they decide whether someone is guilty or not.

    It is their _____.

9. My sister thinks she can _____ everything I should do.

10. This is the place everyone meets for an assembly. _____

Keywords

com•mand—kuh-MAND *verb* 1. to give orders 2. to have control over 3. to demand what you deserve

de•mand—dih-MAND *verb* 1. to ask for something firmly and forcefully 2. to need or require

de•scribe—dih-SKRIB *verb* to use words to tell about the details of someone or something

in•scrip•tion—ihn-SKRIHP-shun *noun* words or letters that are written, printed, or engraved as a lasting record

ma•neu•ver—muh-NOO-vuhr *noun* 1. a skillful move or action 2. a planned movement of military troops or ships 3. an action done to get an advantage

ma•nip•u•late—muh-NIHP-yuh-layt *verb* 1. to operate or use by hand 2. to manage or use with skill 3. to control or influence somebody, usually in order to deceive

man•u•al—MAN-yoo-uhl *adjective* 1. relating to or involving the hands 2. relating to work that requires physical effort 3. operated or powered by human effort

man•u•script—MAN-yuh-skrihpt *noun* 1. a book or document that is written by hand 2. a version of a book, article, or document submitted for publication

scrib•ble—SKRIHB-uhl *verb* to write something quickly and carelessly

sub•scribe—suhb-SKRIB *verb* 1. to pay for something that you will receive over a period of time, such as a magazine 2. to support or give approval to something as if by signing

✓ Check It!

Page 90

Read & Replace

1. subscribe
2. inscription
3. command
4. describe
5. manual
6. manipulate
7. manuscript
8. maneuver
9. scribble
10. demand

Page 91

Root It Out

1. manual
2. inscription
3. command
4. scribble
5. manipulate
6. describe
7. maneuver
8. subscribe
9. demand
10. manuscript

Page 92

Combo Mambo

1. manage: to handle or keep control of something
2. manicure: a treatment for the hands and nails
3. manufacture: to make something into a finished product
4. scripture: sacred writings
5. scriptwriter: someone who writes scripts for a movie or TV show
6. scriptural: relating to sacred writings

Check It!

Read & Replace

The root *man* at the beginning of the word *manual* means *hand*. The root *scribe* at the end of the word *subscribe* means *write*. Read the story. FILL IN the blanks with keywords.

| command | demand | describe | inscription | maneuver |
| manipulate | manual | manuscript | scribble | subscribe |

Jeremy told his grandmother that he wanted to 1_____ to a history magazine. He opened the mailbox and saw the magazine with a card. The 2_____ on the card read, "To Jeremy, with love, Grandma."

On the cover, there was a photo of a general who looked like he was going to 3_____ his men to fight. Inside, Jeremy saw an article that tried to 4_____ what life was like at the time of the Revolutionary War. It told about all the hard 5_____ work the soldiers had to do each day. Jeremy liked the step-by-step photos that showed how blacksmiths used hammers to 6_____ iron. There was also a 7_____ of a general's letter that had been dug up at the battleground, and a diagram of a 8_____ the general had drawn out for his troops.

Jeremy started to 9_____ some notes. He couldn't wait to learn more. He was just going to have to 10_____ that his big sister log off the computer immediately!

Root It Out

LOOK AT each definition. WRITE the missing root letters in the blanks.

HINT: Some roots have alternate spellings.

> *man* = hand   *scribe* = write

1. Work that you need to use your **hands** to do is ___ ___ ___ual labor.

2. Words someone **writes** at the beginning of your book is an

   in ___ ___ ___ ___ ___tion.

3. If you **hand over** orders to someone, you com ___ ___ ___d them.

4. If you **write** quickly and sloppily, you ___ ___ ___ ___ ___ble.

5. You use your **hands** to do this to puzzle pieces: ___ ___ ___ipulate them.

6. When you **write** an e-mail to tell your friend all about your new pet iguana, you

   de ___ ___ ___ ___ ___ ___ it.

7. When you use your **hands** to do a cartwheel, you are doing a gymnastics

   ___ ___ ___euver.

8. When you sign up for **written** materials like a newspaper, you

   sub ___ ___ ___ ___ ___ ___ to it.

9. When you make a forceful or heavy-**handed** request, you

   de ___ ___ ___d something

10. Something that you **write** by **hand** is a ___ ___ ___u___ ___ ___ ___ ___ ___.

Combo Mambo

MATCH a word or ending in a red box to a root in an orange box to make a word. WRITE the word in the root box. Then LOOK UP the definition for each word and WRITE it in a sentence.

man = hand / *scribe* = write

| age | ure | writer | icure | ural | ufacture |

MAN

_____

_____

_____

SCRIB/SCRIPT

_____

_____

_____

_____

_____

_____

_____

_____

_____

_____

_____

Criss Cross

FILL IN the grid by answering the clues with keywords.

ACROSS

2. To ask for firmly

7. To use with skill

8. To write sloppily

9. To pay to have something delivered over a period of time

10. Words that are engraved on something

DOWN

1. Powered by human effort

3. To tell about the details of something

4. To have control over

5. A skillful move

6. A document submitted for publication

Blank Out!

FILL IN the blanks with keywords.

command	demand	describe	inscription	maneuver
manipulate	manual	manuscript	scribble	subscribe

1. Cleaning up your room is a _____ job.

2. A wheelie is a bicycle _____.

3. If you _____ your notes, you may not be able to read them later.

4. Jaden wrote a poem to _____ what it's like to sail.

5. It's not nice to _____ presents for your birthday.

6. Cassie's big brother tried to _____ her into doing his chores.

7. If you _____ to the extreme sports magazine, you'll get a copy every month.

8. When you write a story, make sure to keep a copy of the _____.

9. Zoe had an _____ from her dad on her locket.

10. Brian though he could _____ his little brother to obey him.

It's Puzzling!

MATCH a prefix, root, and suffix together to form a word. Then WRITE the words in the blanks.

HINT: You can use the same prefix, root, or suffix more than once. Some of the ending pieces actually contain more than one suffix.

Prefixes   **Roots**   **Suffixes**

pre-   man   -cipate   _____

_____

_____

un-   script   -er   _____

_____

tran-   scrib   -ion

e-   -age -able

Blank Out!

FILL IN the blanks with keywords.

1. This word tells how you get a newspaper delivered to your home. _____

2. This word is how you tell someone what your best friend looks like.

   _____

3. This word tells what you need to do to get a go-cart to work. _____

4. This word describes a version of a story you send in to be published by a

   magazine. _____

5. When you say, "I want a cookie right now!" you _____ it.

6. This word tells what you might have engraved on your jewelry box.

   _____

7. This word describes how you might doodle in the margin of your paper.

   _____

8. This word tells what you do when you say, "Everyone listen to me!"

   _____

9. When you dig with your hands, you are doing _____ work.

10. Pete used a fancy bike _____ down the tricky hill.

Keywords

gen•der—JEHN-duhr *noun* the male or female group that a person or organism belongs to

gene—JEEN *noun* a basic unit that holds characteristics that are passed from one generation to the next

gen•er•a•tion—jehn-uh-RAY-shuhn *noun* 1. the family members that are a step in line from a single ancestor 2. a group or people born and living at the same time 3. the average length of time it takes for people, animals, or plants to grow up and produce their own offspring

gen•er•ous—JEHN-uhr-uhs *adjective* 1. willing to freely give or share money, help, or time 2. having very high qualities, noble 3. large in size or quantity

in•nate—ih-NAYT *adjective* relating to qualities or abilities that you are born with

na•tion•al•i•ty—NASH-uh-nal-ih-tee *noun* 1. the state of belonging to a country or nation 2. a group of people who have a common beginning, tradition, or language

na•tive—NAY-tihv *adjective* 1. born in a specific place or country 2. born with, or natural 3. grown, made, or having a beginning in a particular region

nat•u•ral—NACH-uhr-uhl *adjective* 1. present in or made by nature, rather than people 2. relating to nature 3. relating to something you are born with 4. not artificial

re•gen•er•ate—rih-JEHN-uh-rayt *verb* 1. to create or produce again 2. to give new life to 3. to replace a lost part with a new growth

su•per•nat•u•ral—soo-puhr-NACH-uhr-uhl *adjective* 1. relating to something that cannot be explained by natural laws 2. outside what is usual or normal

✓ Check It!

Page 98
Read & Replace

1. gene
2. native
3. regenerate
4. innate
5. gender
6. generation
7. generous
8. supernatural
9. nationality
10. natural

Page 99
Root It Out

1. gender
2. innate
3. supernatural
4. generation
5. native
6. natural
7. gene
8. nationality
9. generous
10. regenerate

Page 100
Combo Mambo

1. generate: to bring something into existence
2. genetics: the branch of science that deals with traits inherited through genes
3. genealogy: the study of the history of families
4. nation: a community of people who live in a defined area
5. naturalize: to give citizenship to somebody who is not a native
6. naturally: in a normal manner

Read & Replace

Here are some more roots to add to your collection. The root *gen* at the beginning of the word *gender* means *birth*. The root *nat* in the middle of the word *supernatural* means *born*.

READ the diary entry. FILL IN the blanks with keywords.

gender	gene	generation	generous	innate
nationality	native	natural	regenerate	supernatural

Dear Diary,

My lab experiment was a success! I was finally able to combine the 1 _____ of a pig with one from an iguana. The iguana, a 2 _____ of South America, is able to 3 _____ body parts. The pig is an animal that has 4 _____ intelligence. The new creature, which I call a piguana, makes a great pet. It is smaller than a pig, but it's very smart. If it gets hurt, it can regrow a new part. Soon I'll be able to offer them to pet shops in either 5 _____—male or female. I am excited to be a part of a 6 _____ of scientists who are doing creative lab work. But I couldn't have done this without the 7 _____ help of my assistant, Igor. Some people have called the piguana a monster. They say we have used 8 _____ powers to do our work. Perhaps it is because of my Transylvanian 9 _____. But these claims are untrue. It is completely 10 _____ to want to push science to its limits.

Dr. Frankenfeld

Root It Out

READ each definition. WRITE the missing root letters in the blanks.

HINT: Some roots have alternate spellings.

gen = birth   *nat* = born

gender	gene	generation	generous	innate
nationality	native	natural	regenerate	supernatural

1. Whether you're a girl or boy at **birth**, that's your ___ ___ ___ der.

2. An ability you were **born** with is in ___ ___ ___ ___.

3. Something that is **born** outside of natural laws is considered

   super ___ ___ ___ ural.

4. A group of people that share similar **birth** years are part of a ___ ___ ___ eration.

5. Someone who was **born** in this country is a ___ ___ ___ ive.

6. Something that is **born** in nature and not created in a lab is ___ ___ ___ ural.

7. Scientists are trying to figure out if a ___ ___ ___ e you have at **birth** can

   determine if you might get a disease.

8. A group of people who were **born** in a common place have the same

   ___ ___ ___ ionality.

9. If you have a noble spirit from **birth**, you are ___ ___ ___ erous.

10. To regrow or give **birth** to a lost part: re ___ ___ ___ erate

Combo Mambo

MATCH a word or ending in a blue box to a root in a green box to make a word. WRITE the word in the root box. Then LOOK UP the definition for each word and WRITE it in a sentence.

erate   ion   uralize   etics   urally   ealogy

GEN
_____
_____
_____

NAT
_____
_____
_____

Criss Cross

FILL IN the grid by answering the clues with keywords.

ACROSS

2. The length of time between the birth of parents and the birth of their offspring
4. Outside of what is normal
5. Not artificial
6. Born in a particular place

DOWN

1. The part of DNA that holds information that has been passed down from each parent
3. To create again
5. The state of belonging to a nation

Blank Out!

FILL IN the blanks with keywords.

gender	gene	generation	generous	innate
nationality	native	natural	regenerate	supernatural

1. Fred prefers _____ juice to the kind made with artificial flavors.

2. Brenda believes she has _____ powers and can read other people's minds.

3. Does a _____ determine whether you are shy or not?

4. Nestor's dad was a piano player, so his musical ability must be _____.

5. It is very _____ to give your bed to your sister's friend during a sleepover party.

6. Chloe had a flag printed on her T-shirt to show her _____.

7. An iguana can _____ a new tail.

8. A new _____ of extreme athletes is ready to compete with the older crowd.

9. There are male and female athletes, so people of either _____ can be great athletes.

10. We asked Kevin to show us around New York City because he is a _____ New Yorker.

It's Puzzling!

MATCH a prefix, root, and suffix together to form a word. Then WRITE the words in the blanks.

HINT: If you get stuck, use a dictionary. Some of the ending pieces actually contain more than one suffix.

Prefixes   **Roots**   **Suffixes**

patho-   nat   -al   _____

pre-   gen   -ic

inter-   -ion -al

Blank Out!

FILL IN the blanks with keywords.

1. Orange juice that you squeezed from an orange is _____.

2. The difference between men and women is _____.

3. Some animals _____ a limb when they need to grow a new one.

4. All of the kids in your grade are a part of the same _____.

5. If you are a great tennis player, just like your mother, the ability is

   _____.

6. If you still live in the town where you were born, you're a _____.

7. Ghosts and goblins are _____.

8. Citizenship is another word for _____.

9. Your eye color is determined by a _____.

10. If you give all your old baseball cards to your sister, you are _____.

Keywords

de•fine—dih-FIN *verb* 1. to give a precise meaning of 2. to describe something clearly 3. to mark the limits of

def•i•nite—DEHF-uh-niht *adjective* 1. having fixed limits 2. clear in meaning 3. certain and unlikely to change plans

fi•nal•ize—FI-nuh-liz *verb* to put in final form

fi•nite—FI-nit *adjective* 1. with an end or limit 2. with a countable number of parts

il•lit•er•ate—IH-liht-uhr-iht *adjective* 1. having little or no education 2. being unable to read

in•fi•nite—IHN-fuh-niht *adjective* 1. without any limits or end 2. immeasurably great in size or number

lit•er•a•cy—LIHT-uhr-uh-see *noun* the ability to read and write

lit•er•al—LIHT-uhr-uhl *adjective* 1. true to fact 2. following the usual meaning of words 3. done word for word

lit•er•ar•y—LIHT-uh-rehr-ee *adjective* 1. relating to written works or writing as a profession 2. well read

lit•er•a•ture—LIHT-uhr-uh-choor *noun* written works such as books, poetry, and plays that are known for their excellence

✓ Check It!

Page 106

Read & Replace

1. literature
2. illiterate
3. infinite
4. definite
5. literal
6. literary
7. define
8. finalize
9. literacy
10. finite

Page 107

Root It Out

1. literature
2. define
3. literary
4. finite
5. literacy
6. finalize
7. illiterate
8. literal
9. infinite
10. definite

Page 108

Combo Mambo

1. finalist: someone who gets to the final rounds of a competition
2. finish: to come to an end
3. finally: after a long period of time
4. literalism: sticking strictly to the basic meaning of a word or story
5. literal: the exact meaning of a word
6. literalize: to make literal

Page 109

Criss Cross

ACROSS	DOWN
2. illiterate	1. define
5. definite	3. infinite
7. finalize	4. literal
8. literacy	6. literary

Roots, Last Call!

✓ Check It!

Page 110

Blank Out!

1. define
2. literal
3. literature
4. finalize
5. literary
6. illiterate
7. definite
8. finite
9. literacy
10. infinite

Page 111

It's Puzzling!

alliteration
definition
infinity
obliterate
obliteration

Page 112

Blank Out!

1. infinite
2. illiterate
3. definite
4. finalize
5. finite
6. literature
7. literal
8. literacy
9. literary
10. define

Read & Replace

The root *fin* in the middle of the word *definite* means *end*. The root *liter* at the beginning of the word *literature* means *letters*. Read the script. FILL IN the blanks with keywords.

define	definite	finalize	finite	infinite
illiterate	literal	literary	literature	literacy

Johnny: Hello?

Salesperson: Hi. I have a collection of fine 1_____ that I'd like to offer you today.

Johnny: No thank you. I'm 2_____, so I can't read.

Salesperson: But there are an 3_____ number of uses for this collection. You can use them as hot plates.

Johnny: I'm sorry, but my answer is a 4_____ no.

Salesperson: You're only thinking about the 5_____ meaning of my words. With this collection, you'll look like a real 6_____ genius.

Johnny: Do I have to 7_____ no for you?

Salesperson: Let's just 8_____this deal now. You seem like you really need these books.

Johnny: Look, it's great that you care about 9_____.
I was only joking, I can read well.
But I have a 10_____
amount of patience. [click]

Root It Out

LOOK AT each definition. WRITE the missing root letters in the blanks.

1. Writers use **letters** to create these great books. ___ ___ ___ ___ ___ ature

2. When you mark the **end** or boundary of a space, you de ___ ___ ___ e it.

3. If you work by writing **letters**, words, and sentences, you have this kind of job.

   ___ ___ ___ ___ ___ ary

4. Every year has an **end** so it is ___ ___ ___ ite.

5. The skills you need to put **letters** together to read words.

   ___ ___ ___ ___ ___ acy

6. When your conversation comes to an **end** and you agree on a decision.

   fin ___ ___ ___ ___ ___ it.

7. If someone does not know the **letters** of the alphabet and cannot read, she is

   il ___ ___ ___ ___ ___ ate.

8. If you read the **letters** of a word and only think about its exact meaning, you are

   being ___ ___ ___ ___ ___ al.

9. You can't finish counting numbers without an **end** because they are

   in ___ ___ ___ ite.

10. If you can clearly see the **ends** of something, it is de ___ ___ ___ ite.

Combo Mambo

MATCH a word or ending in a blue box to a root in a red box to make a word. WRITE the word in the root box. Then LOOK UP the definition for each word and WRITE the word in a sentence.

fin = end   *liter* = letters

alist	alism	al	ish	ally	eralize

FIN	LITER
_____	_____
_____	_____
_____	_____

_____

_____

_____

_____

_____

_____

_____

Criss Cross

FILL IN the grid by answering the clues with keywords.

ACROSS

2. Not able to read
5. Unlikely to change
7. To put in finished form
8. The ability to read and write

DOWN

1. To mark the limits of
3. Without limits
4. Exactly as said or written
6. Well-read

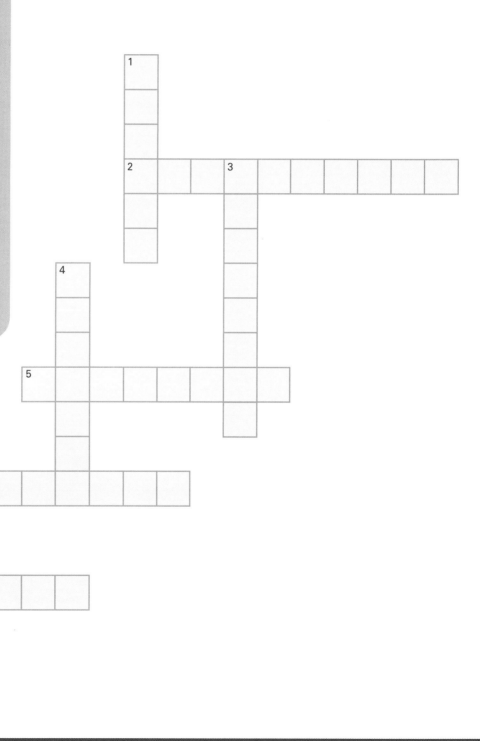

Blank Out!

FILL IN the blanks with keywords.

| define | definite | finalize | finite | infinite |
| illiterate | literal | literary | literature | literacy |

1. If you draw a line in the middle of the room that your brother cannot cross, you

   _____ a boundary.

2. If a friend takes what you say word for word and doesn't understand that you are

   joking, he is being _____.

3. If you read great works of _____, you'll be considered well read.

4. Victoria was waiting to _____ her plans before giving Joe an answer.

5. An author has a _____ profession.

6. Hans volunteered as a tutor to help teach _____ adults learn to read.

7. If you know that you will absolutely, positively do something, you are

   _____ that you will do it.

8. If you can see both ends of a line, it is _____.

9. If you talk about the number of kids

   you know who can read, you are talking

   about your friends' _____.

10. Walter has an _____

    amount of love for his grandpa.

It's Puzzling!

MATCH a prefix, root, and suffix together to form a word. Then WRITE the words in the blanks.

HINT: You can use the same prefix, root, or suffix more than once.

Prefixes   **Roots**   **Suffixes**

de-   liter   -ity

_____

_____

al-   fin   -ation

_____

_____

in-   -ate

_____

ob-   -ition

Roots, Last Call!

Blank Out!

FILL IN the blanks with keywords.

define	definite	finalize	finite	infinite
illiterate	literal	literary	literature	literacy

1. This word tells how many grains of sand there are on the beach.

   _____

2. This word describes someone who does not know how to read.

   _____

3. If you have no doubts about going to the movie on Friday, your plans are

   _____.

4. This word is what you do when you decide with your friends exactly what movie

   you will see. _____

5. This word describes the number of days in a year. _____

6. This word describes the written works in a library. _____

7. This word describes the meaning of something exactly as it is written.

   _____

8. This word means the ability to read and write. _____

9. This word describes the type of person you are if you read a lot of books.

   _____

10. This word tells what you do when you say what a word means. _____

Pick the One!

You know your root words, right? So get going and check your skills! LOOK AT each group of words. CIRCLE the actual English word in each row.

1.	audible	audograph	inaudate
2.	dictalize	dictator	dictite
3.	unnational	nationor	nationality
4.	geneful	generation	genation
5.	nonsense	subsense	unsense
6.	maniture	manipulate	maniscribe
7.	illiterate	unliterate	reliterate
8.	infinite	prefinite	disfinite

Combo Mambo

WRITE all the words you can make by adding the suffixes to the roots.

HINT: Some roots are used more than once.

Root

fin

aud

liter

dict

Suffix

ite

ate

al

ible

ator

ition

_____

_____

_____

_____

_____

_____

_____

Match Up!

Can you MATCH each root to its meaning? When you're done, WRITE three words that contain each root.

1. aud ___   a. hand

2. dict ___   b. birth

3. script ___   c. letters

4. man ___   d. end

5. nat ___   e. write

6. gen ___   f. hear

7. litera ___   g. born

8. fin ___   h. say

1. _____ _____ _____

2. _____ _____ _____

3. _____ _____ _____

4. _____ _____ _____

5. _____ _____ _____

6. _____ _____ _____

7. _____ _____ _____

8. _____ _____ _____

Pathfinder

The game's the same, only the roots change. Begin at START. When you get to a box with two arrows, pick the root that you can add to the prefix. If you make all the right choices, you'll end up at FINISH.

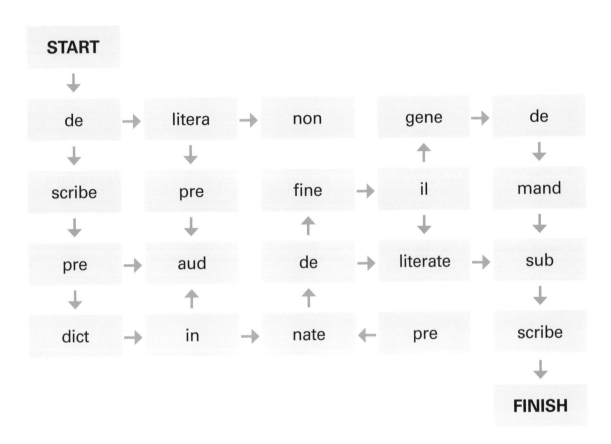

Sniglets!

You're not quite finished with sniglets yet! Here are some sniglets made with the roots you just reviewed.

litermature–the ability to read books that are challenging for your age
manibrate–the buzzing of a video game controller in your hand
audilogue–the conversation that happens when you talk to yourself
marscription–the doodles you write in the margins of your notebook
finifood–a bedtime snack, or the last thing you eat each day
genolit–the most popular books in a certain age group

WRITE a sniglet from the list to complete each sentence.

1. Choose your own adventures were the _____ ten years ago.

2. Samantha spent so much time on her _____ she forgot to take notes.

3. Cookies and milk are my favorite _____.

4. It was embarrassing when Quentin overheard my _____.

5. Martin is reading Shakespeare. That's very _____.

6. Sometimes the _____ can be distracting when you're playing a game.

Now it's your turn. Here are some prefixes and roots you can use to create more sniglets.

Prefix	Root
ante- = before	hydro = water
contra- = against	matri = mother
hyper- = over, above	tempo = time
tele- = distance, from afar	vac = empty

ac•quire—uh-KWIR *verb* 1. to get as your own 2. to gain for yourself. Synonyms: get, gain, obtain. Antonyms: provide, give.

ap•proach—uh-PROHCH *verb* 1. to move closer to; 2. to speak to someone in order to ask something. Synonyms: advance, move toward. Antonyms: retreat, pull back.

au•di•ble—AW-duh-buhl *adjective* able to be heard

au•di•ence—AW-dee-uhns *noun* a group that listens or watches

au•di•o—AW-dee-oh *adjective* 1. relating to sound that can be heard 2. relating to the recording or reproduction of sound

au•di•tion—aw-DIHSH-uhn *noun* 1. the sense of hearing 2. a test performance by a musician, singer, dancer, or actor

au•di•to•ri•um—awd-ih-TOHR-ee-uhm *noun* a building, or the area of a building, where the audience sits

bare—BAYR *adjective* 1. naked 2. exposed for all to see 3. empty

bear—BAYR *noun* a large mammal that has long shaggy hair and a short tail and eats both plants and meat *verb* 1. to hold up something heavy 2. to keep in one's mind

ben•e•fi•cial—behn-uh-FIHSH-uhl *adjective* 1. helpful; 2. leading to good health and happiness. Synonyms: helpful, useful. Antonyms: harmful, destructive.

bright•ly—BRIT-lee *adverb* 1. in a way that gives off a lot of light 2. in a way that seems happy and cheerful

care•less—KAYR-lihs *adjective* 1. not paying careful attention to 2. done, made, or said without care

com•mand—kuh-MAND *verb* 1. to give orders 2. to have control over 3. to demand what you deserve

con•tent¹—kuhn-TEHNT *adjective* satisfied with what you have

con•tent²—KAHN-tehnt *noun* 1. the amount of something inside something else 2. the subject or topic covered 3. the meaning or truth of a creative work

con•tract¹—KAHN-trakt *noun* 1. a legal agreement between two or more people or groups

con•tract²—kuhn-TRAKT *verb* 1. to draw or squeeze together 2. to shorten or make smaller

damp•ness—DAMP-nuhs *noun* the quality of being slightly wet

de•fine—dih-FIN *verb* 1. to give a precise meaning of 2. to describe something clearly 3. to mark the limits of

def•i•nite—DEHF-uh-niht *adjective* 1. having fixed limits 2. clear in meaning 3. certain and unlikely to change plans

de•mand—dih-MAND *verb* 1. to ask for something firmly and forcefully 2. to need or require

de•scribe—dih-SKRIB *verb* to use words to tell about the details of someone or something

des•ert¹—DEHZ-uhrt *noun* a land that is dry and has few plants

de•sert²—dih-ZUHRT *verb* 1. to go away from 2. to leave someone that you should stay with 3. to quit and leave without permission

dic•tate—DIHK-tayt *verb* 1. to speak or read for someone to write down 2. to give orders or rule over

dic•ta•tor—DIHK-tay-ter *noun* a leader who rules with total power over others

dic•tion•ar•y—DIHK-shuh-nehr-ee *noun* a reference book that lists words in alphabetical order and explains their meanings

dis•hon•est—dihs-OHN-ihst *adjective* lying, not honest

dis•please—dihs-PLEEZ *verb* to make someone feel dislike or annoyance

dis•sim•i•lar—dih-SIHM-uh-luhr *adjective* different, unlike

end•less—EHND-lihs *adjective* 1. without end or limits 2. joined at the ends

e•nor•mous—ih-NAWR-muhs *adjective* unusually large in size or number. Synonyms: huge, massive, gigantic. Antonyms: tiny, small.

Index

en•ter•tain•ment—en-tuhr-TAYN-muhnt *noun* ways to give pleasure to or amuse people, such as singing, dancing, and acting

fair—FAYR *noun* 1. a gathering of people who are buying and selling things 2. an event with rides, games, and competitions.
adjective 1. beautiful 2. clean or pure 3. not stormy or cloudy 4. likely to happen 5. not dark 6. neither good nor bad 7. in a way that is equal for everyone involved

fare—FAYR *noun* 1. food 2. the money a person pays to travel by public transportation

fear•ful—FEER-fuhl *adjective* 1. causing fear 2. filled with fear 3. nervous and easily frightened

feath•er•y—FEHTH-uh-ree *adjective* 1. like a feather 2. covered in feathers

fi•nal•ize—FI-nuh-liz *verb* to put in final form

fi•nal•ly—FIN-uhl-ee *adverb* 1. after a long period of time 2. happening at the end or last

fi•nite—FI-nit *adjective* 1. with an end or limit 2. with a countable number of parts

frac•ture—FRAK-cher *verb* to break. Synonyms: break, crack, rupture. Antonyms: fix, mend.

gen•der—JEHN-duhr *noun* the male or female group that a person or organism belongs to

gene—JEEN *noun* a basic unit that holds characteristics that are passed from one generation to the next

gen•er•a•tion—jehn-uh-RAY-shuhn *noun* 1. the family members that are a step in line from a single ancestor 2. a group or people born and living at the same time 3. the average length of time it takes for people, animals, or plants to grow up and produce their own offspring

gen•er•ous—JEHN-uhr-uhs *adjective* 1. willing to freely give or share money, help, or time 2. having very high qualities, noble 3. large in size or quantity

gloom•y—GLOO-mee *adjective* 1. dark 2. sad. Synonyms: dark, unhappy, sad. Antonyms: bright, cheerful.

grad•u•al—GRAJ-ooh-uhl *adjective* moving or changing slowly in steps or degrees
Synonyms: slow, steady, regular. Antonyms: sudden, fast.

grate•ful—GRAYT-fuhl *adjective* having the desire to thank someone

heal—HEEL *verb* to make healthy

heel—HEEL *noun* 1. the back part of the foot below the ankle 2. the part of a shoe that covers the back of the foot 3. the lower, back, or end part 4. a person who is not nice. *verb* to make a person or animal obey

hu•mor•ous—HYOO-mer-uhs *adjective* funny. Synonyms: amusing, hilarious, funny. Antonyms: serious.

il•lit•er•ate—IH-liht-uhr-iht *adjective* 1. having little or no education 2. being unable to read

im•prove—ihm-PROOV *adjective* to make or become better. Synonyms: get better, recover. Antonyms: worsen, deteriorate.

in•fi•nite—IHN-fuh-niht *adjective* 1. without any limits or end 2. immeasurably great in size or number

in•nate—ih-NAYT *adjective* relating to qualities or abilities that you are born with

in•quire—ihn-KWIR *verb* to ask about. Synonyms: ask, request. Antonyms: respond.

in•scrip•tion—ihn-SKRIHP-shun *noun* words or letters that are written, printed, or engraved as a lasting record

lit•er•a•cy—LIHT-uhr-uh-see *noun* the ability to read and write

lit•er•al—LIHT-uhr-uhl *adjective* 1. true to fact 2. following the usual meaning of words 3. done word for word

lit•er•ar•y—LIHT-uh-rehr-ee *adjective* 1. relating to written works or writing as a profession 2. well read

lit•er•a•ture—LIHT-uhr-uh-choor *noun* written works such as books, poetry, and plays that are known for their excellence

lo•cate—LOH-kayt *verb* 1. to find where something is; 2. to put in a particular spot. Synonyms: place, find, discover. Antonyms: lose, misplace.

loud•ness—LOWD-nuhs *noun* 1. the degree of volume of sound

ma•neu•ver—muh-NOO-vuhr *noun* 1. a skillful move or action 2. a planned movement of military troops or ships 3. an action done to get an advantage

ma•nip•u•late—muh-NIHP-yuh-layt *verb* 1. to operate or use by hand 2. to manage or use with skill 3. to control or influence somebody, usually in order to deceive

man•u•al—MAN-yoo-uhl *adjective* 1. relating to or involving the hands 2. relating to work that requires physical effort 3. operated or powered by human effort

man•u•fac•ture—man-yuh-FAK-cher *verb* to make by hand or with machinery. Synonyms: make, produce, create. Antonyms: destroy, demolish.

man•u•script—MAN-yuh-skrihpt *noun* 1. a book or document that is written by hand 2. a version of a book, article, or document submitted for publication

mend—mend *verb* 1. to fix 2. to make better. Synonyms: repair, fix, recover. Antonyms: break, fracture.

mi•nus•cule—MIHN-uh-skyool *adjective* very small. Synonyms: tiny, minute, little. Antonyms: enormous, gigantic.

move•ment—MOOV-muhnt *noun* 1. the act of changing location or position 2. the way in which somebody or something moves

na•tion•al•i•ty—NASH-uh-nal-ih-tee *noun* 1. the state of belonging to a country or nation 2. a group of people who have a common beginning, tradition, or language

na•tive—NAY-tihv *adjective* 1. born in a specific place or country 2. born with, or natural 3. grown, made, or having a beginning in a particular region

nat•u•ral—NACH-uhr-uhl *adjective* 1. present in or made by nature, rather than people 2. relating to nature 3. relating to something you are born with 4. not artificial

non•mov•ing—nahn-MOO-vihng *adjective* in a fixed position, not changing place or position

non•sense—NAHN-sehnts *noun* silly or meaningless words or actions

non•tox•ic—nahn-TAHK-sihk *adjective* not poisonous, harmless

o•rig•i•nal—uh-RIHJ-uh-nuhl *adjective* 1. existing first 2. completely new and not copied. Synonyms: first, earliest, new. Antonyms: final, copy.

ob•ject¹—OHB-jehkt *noun* 1. something that you can see and touch 2. something that is the target of your thoughts or feelings 3. the reason for doing something

ob•ject²—ohb-JEHKT *verb* to go against or oppose with firm words

pain•less—PAYN-lihs *adjective* 1. not causing pain 2. involving little difficulty

play•ful—PLAY-fuhl *adjective* 1. full of play, fond of playing 2. said or done in a fun way

pre•cau•tion—prih-CAW-shun *noun* something done beforehand to prevent harm

pre•dict—prih-DIHKT *verb* to tell what is going to happen in the future

pre•his•tor•ic—pree-hih-STAWR-ihk *adjective* relating to something that happened before written history

pre•school—PREE-skool *noun* the school a child attends before elementary school

pres•ent¹—PREHZ-uhnt *noun* 1. something that is given to another 2. time that is happening now

pre•sent²—prih-ZEHNT *verb* 1. to introduce, to bring out before a group of people 2. to give

pre•view—PREE-vyoo *verb* to show or look at in advance

pro•vide—pruh-VID *verb* 1. to take care of 2. to supply what is needed. Synonyms: give, offer, supply. Antonyms: get, take.

pun•ish•ment—PUHN-ihsh-muhnt *noun* the act of punishing 2. a penalty for wrongdoing 3. rough treatment

re•ar•range—ree-uh-RAYNJ *verb* to put things in a new order or position

re•cent•ly—REES-uhnt-lee *adverb* relating to a time not long ago

Index

re•gen•er•ate—rih-JEHN-uh-rayt *verb* 1. to create or produce again 2. to give new life to 3. to replace a lost part with a new growth

re•play—REE-play *verb* to play again

re•spond—rih-SPAHND *verb* 1. to answer 2. to react in response. Synonyms: reply, answer. Antonyms: ask, question.

re•view—REE-vyoo *verb* 1. to look at again 2. to report on the quality of something 3. to study or check again

scent—SEHNT *noun* 1. an odor or smell 2. a sense of smell 3. hint 4. perfume

scrib•ble—SKRIHB-uhl *verb* to write something quickly and carelessly

sent—SEHNT *verb* 1. caused to go 2. caused to happen

shad•ow•y—SHAD-oh-ee *adjective* 1. full of shadows 2. not clearly seen 3. not realistic

sly•ness—SLI-nuhs *noun* the quality of being sneaky or smart at hiding one's goals

sneak•y—SNEE-kee *adjective* doing things in a secret and sometimes unfair way

speed•i•ly—SPEED-uhl-ee *adverb* with quickness

sub•ma•rine—suhb-muh-REEN *noun* a vehicle that operates underwater

sub•scribe—suhb-SKRIB *verb* 1. to pay for something that you will receive over a period of time, such as a magazine 2. to support or give approval to something as if by signing

sub•top•ic—SUHB-tahp-ihk *noun* a topic that is a part of the main topic

sub•way—SUHB-way *noun* 1. a passage underneath the ground 2. an underground railway

suf•fi•cient—suh-FISH-uhnt *adjective* as much as needed. Synonyms: enough, plenty, ample. Antonyms: inadequate, poor.

su•per•nat•u•ral—soo-puhr-NACH-uhr-uhl *adjective* 1. relating to something that cannot be explained by natural laws 2. outside what is usual or normal

truth•ful—TROOTH-fuhl *adjective* honest, true, always telling the truth

un•com•fort•a•ble—uhn-CUHM-fert-uh-bul *adjective* not feeling or giving comfort

un•like•ly—uhn-LIK-lee *adjective* not likely to happen

un•lim•it•ed—uhn-LIH-mih-tuhd *adjective* 1. without limits 2. having no boundaries or end. Synonyms: boundless, limitless. Antonyms: confined, bound.

un•u•su•al—uhn-YOO-zhoo-wuhl *adjective* not common, rare

un•wise—uhn-WIZ *adjective* not wise, foolish

van•ish—VAN-ihsh *verb* 1. to disappear suddenly 2. to stop existing. Synonyms: disappear, go. Antonyms: appear, show.

ver•dict—VUHR-dihkt *noun* 1. the decision a jury reaches together 2. an opinion about something

weak—WEEK *adjective* not strong

week—WEEK *noun* the period of seven days that begins with Sunday and ends with Saturday